Contents

Part I

THE LOGIC OF FAILURE

Part II

COGNITIVE DISSONANCE

Vol.2

Part II
COGNITIVE DISSONANCE

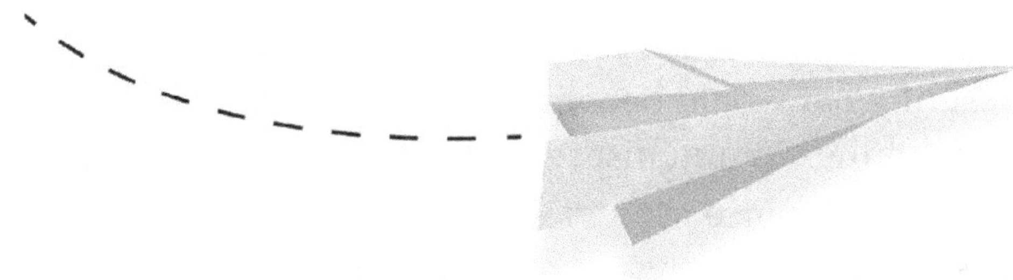

Chapter 6

Reforming Criminal Justice

I

Trofim Lysenko was a dark-haired, bright-eyed biologist. He came from peasant stock in the west of what would become the Soviet Union and was spotted by the political leaders of the Communist revolution in the 1920s, when he claimed to have found a way to enhance crop yields.[1]

The technique was not as successful as Lysenko claimed, but the young scientist was ambitious and politically savvy. Over a period of ten years he gradually moved up the academic ranks. In 1934, he was appointed to the Lenin All-Union Academy of Agricultural Sciences.

It was then that he took a major gamble. In the early twentieth century, the science of genetics, based on the work of Gregor Mendel, a German friar and scientist, was just beginning to take off. It proposed that heredity was encoded in small units called genes and could be described using statistical rules. Lysenko became an outspoken critic of this new theory, positioning himself against a rising tide of scientific opinion.

Lysenko was not stupid. He calculated that this stance would endear him further to the political elite. Marxism was based on the idea that human nature is malleable. Genetics, which held that certain traits are passed down from generation to generation, seemed like a threat to this doctrine. Lysenko started to defend a different idea: the notion that traits acquired during one's lifetime could be passed on. It is sometimes called Lamarckism, after the original proponent of the theory.

Scientific ideas should succeed or fail according to rational argument and evidence. It is about data rather than dogma. But Lysenko realized that he couldn't silence the geneticists through argument alone. Thousands of scientists up and down the country were excited by the new genetic approach. They sincerely believed that it had intellectual merit and that it should, therefore, be pursued. And they had data to back up their beliefs.

So Lysenko tried a different approach: instead of engaging in debate, he tried to shut it down. He called upon Stalin to outlaw the new theory of genetics. Stalin agreed, not because genetics had been proved wanting scientifically, but because it didn't tally with Communist ideology. Together they declared genetics "a bourgeois perversion." The ideas of Lamarck, on the other hand, were given the Communist seal of approval.

Those who dissented from the Party line were ruthlessly persecuted. Many geneticists were executed, including Israel Agol, Solomon Levit, Grigorii Levitskii, Georgii Karpechenko, and Georgii Nadson, or sent to labor camps. Nikolai Vavilov, one of the most eminent Soviet scientists, was arrested in 1940 and died in prison in 1943. All genetic research was forbidden and at scientific meetings around the country geneticists were condemned and dismissed.

Lysenko had silenced his critics and pretty much guaranteed that his own ideas would triumph. But this "success" had a familiar sting in its tail. By protecting his ideas from dissent, he had deprived them of a valuable thing: the possibility of failure. He proposed all sorts of techniques to improve crop yields, but nobody tested them out of fear of persecution. Science had effectively been detached, by political decree, from the feedback mechanism of falsification.

The results were devastating. Before the rise of Lysenko, Russian biology had been flourishing. Dmitry Ivanovsky discovered plant viruses in 1892. Ivan Pavlov won the Nobel Prize for Medicine in 1904 for his work on digestion. Ilya Mechnikov won the Nobel Prize in 1908 for his theories on the cellular response to infection. In 1927, Nikolai Koltsov proposed that inherited characteristics are double-stranded giant molecules, anticipating the double helix structure of DNA.

By the end of the purges, however, Russian science had been decimated. As Valery Soyfer, a Russian scientist persecuted during the Lysenko era, put it: "The progress of science was slowed or stopped, and millions of university and high school students received a distorted education."[2] This produced a ripple effect on the quality of life for millions of Russians, not least because the agricultural techniques proposed by Lysenko were often ineffective. This is what happens when ideas are not allowed to fail.

For Communist China, which had also embraced Lysenko's ideas, the results were, in many ways, even more catastrophic. Lysenko had publicly come out in favor of a technique of close planting of crop seeds in order to increase output.

The theory was that plants of the same species would not compete with each other for nutrients.

This fitted in with Marxist and Maoist ideas about organisms from the same class living in harmony rather than in competition. "With company, they grow easy," Mao told colleagues. "When they grow together, they will be comfortable." The Chinese leader drew up an eight-point Lysenko-inspired blueprint for the Great Leap Forward, and persecuted Western-trained scientists and geneticists with the same kind of ferocity as in the Soviet Union.[3]

The theory of close-planting should have been put to the test. It should have been subject to possible failure. Instead it was adopted on ideological grounds. "In Southern China, a density of 1.5 million seedlings per 2.5 acres was usually the norm," Jasper Becker writes in *Hungry Ghosts, Mao's Secret Famine*. "But in 1958, peasants were ordered to plant 6.5 million per 2.5 acres."

Too late, it was discovered that the seeds did indeed compete with each other, stunting growth and damaging yields. It contributed to one of the worst disasters in Chinese history, a tragedy that even now has not been fully revealed. Historians estimate that between 20 and 43 million people died during one of the most devastating famines in human history.

• • •

The Lysenko incident is rightly regarded as one of the most scandalous episodes in the history of science. It has been the subject of dozens of books (including the magisterial *Lysenko and the Tragedy of Soviet Science*), hundreds of journal articles, and it is familiar to almost all researchers. It serves as a stark warning about the dangers of protecting ideas from the possibility of failure.

Yet a different and more subtle form of the Lysenko tendency exists in the world today. Ideas and beliefs of all kinds are protected from failure, but not by a totalitarian state. Instead they are protected from failure *by us*.

Cognitive dissonance doesn't leave a paper trail. There are no documents that can be pointed to when we reframe inconvenient truths. There is no violence perpetrated by the state or anyone else. It is a process of *self*-deception. And this can have devastating effects, not least on those who were the subject of chapter 4: the wrongly convicted.

And this brings us back to the DNA exoneration era. We have seen that these cases were difficult for the police and prosecutors to accept. But to close this section, let us explore these graphic failures in the criminal justice system and see what they tell us about how the system should be reformed to prevent them from ever happening again.

The answer, it turns out, starts with creating a system that is sensitive to the inherent flaws in human memory.[*]

II

Neil deGrasse Tyson is an eminent astrophysicist, popular science writer, and media personality. He has eighteen honorary doctorates and was once voted the sexiest astrophysicist in the world. He is also a prolific public speaker. Many of his performances are on YouTube.

For many years after 9/11, Tyson told a particular story about George W. Bush. The former president had made a speech in the days after the attack on the twin towers. Tyson quoted Bush as saying in this speech: "Our God is the God who named the stars."[4]

To Tyson this was a destructive thing for the president to say. He felt that Bush was seeking to divide Christians and Muslims in the aftermath of an attack by Islamic extremists. It was an insinuation that Christians believed in the true God, given that He had named the stars.

As Tyson put it: "George Bush, within a week of [the attacks], gave us a speech attempting to distinguish 'we' from 'they.' And who are 'they'? These were the Muslim fundamentalists . . . And how does he do it? He says . . . 'Our God is the God who named the stars.'"

But Tyson wasn't finished. Bush was not just being bigoted, he said, but also inaccurate. In the next sentence Tyson revealed that two thirds of identified stars actually have Arabic names, having been discovered by Muslim scholars. "I don't think Bush knew this," Tyson said. "That would confound the point he was making."

The speech was highly effective. It mesmerized audiences and made an acute political point. It also positioned Bush as an irresponsible president, using a tragedy to divide Americans at a moment of great sensitivity. But there was a small problem. When a journalist from the Federalist website went looking for the Bush quote, he couldn't find it. He searched the TV and newspaper archives for the statements of the president after 9/11, but the "stars quote" didn't seem to be there.[5]

When Tyson was contacted, he was adamant that he could remember Bush making the statement. "I have explicit memory of those words being spoken by the President," he said. "I reacted on the spot, making a note for possible later reference in my public discourse. Odd that nobody seems to be able to find the quote anywhere."

But no matter how hard journalists looked for it, they couldn't find it. The only speech that Bush had made in the aftermath of the attacks had been very different from the one highlighted by Tyson. "The enemy of America is not our many Muslim friends," Bush said. "It is not our many Arab friends. Our enemy is a radical network of terrorists and every government that supports them." This was reconciliatory, and as for stars, he didn't mention them at all.

Only later did researchers uncover a quote where Bush *did* mention stars, but it wasn't made after 9/11; it was spoken in the aftermath of the Space Shuttle *Columbia* disaster. "The same creator who names the stars also knows the names of the seven souls we mourn today," Bush said.

Needless to say, this put an entirely different gloss on the quote, and made something of a mockery of Tyson's interpretation. This was a president offering words of comfort and hope for the families of those who had died in the *Columbia* tragedy—and he was making no contrast with Islam.

But Tyson was nothing if not insistent. He said that he had a clear memory of Bush saying the words after 9/11. For a while, he wouldn't budge. Only after weeks of being asked to find a scrap of evidence for the original quote did he finally issue a retraction. "I here publicly apologize to the President for casting his quote in the context of contrasting religions rather than as a poetic reference to the lost souls of *Columbia*,"[6] he said.

The post-9/11 "stars" speech by George W. Bush never happened.

This episode is revealing because it shows that even practicing scientists are suckers for the seemingly inviolable power of memory. When we remember seeing something, it feels as if we are accessing a videotape of a real, tangible, rock-solid event. It feels like it *must* have happened. When people question one's memory it is natural to get irate.

But Tyson is not the first to have created a fictitious memory. In a study in Scotland, members of the public were adamant that they could remember a nurse removing a skin sample from their little finger. But this never happened. A week earlier these volunteers had been asked by researchers to *imagine* a nurse removing the sample. But somehow, on recollection, it had morphed into a real event. They were four times as likely to recall it as real compared with those who had not been asked to imagine it.[7]

In a different study, volunteers were asked to look at films of car bumpers in which no windows or headlights were broken. Later, they were asked how fast the cars were going when they "smashed" into each other. Suddenly they started reporting memories of glass shattering when no glass had smashed at all. They had reengineered the memory to encompass the new information provided by the word "smashed."[8]

Memory, it turns out, is not as reliable as we think. We do not encode high-definition movies of our experiences and then access them at will. Rather, memory is a system dispersed throughout the brain and is subject to all sorts of biases. Memories are suggestible. We often assemble fragments of entirely different experiences and weave them together into what seems like a coherent whole. With each recollection, we engage in editing.*

By retrieving, editing, and integrating disparate memories, we have imagined an entirely new event. People with amnesia, however, are unable to do this. They struggle to remember the past, but they also cannot imagine the future.

In short, the very fact that memory is so malleable may lead us astray when it comes to recollection. But it could also play a crucial role in imagining and anticipating future events.

We try to make the memory fit with what we now know rather than what we once saw. In the case of Jean Charles de Menezes, for example, who was shot by police in an Underground station in the aftermath of the London terrorist atrocities in 2005, eyewitnesses said that he had been wearing a bulky jacket, had run away from police, and had vaulted a ticket barrier.

But it turned out that all of this was untrue. Menezes, an innocent passenger, was actually "wearing a light denim shirt or jacket, walked through the barriers having picked up a free newspaper, and only ran when he saw his train arriving."[9] The witnesses had transposed what they had seen with what they had read about the event subsequently in the newspapers.

With this in mind it will not seem surprising that when the Innocence Project started to investigate the signatures of wrongful convictions, they discovered that mistaken eyewitness identification was a contributing factor in an astonishing 75 percent of cases.[10] People were testifying in open court that they had seen people at the scene of a crime who in fact were elsewhere at the time.

These witnesses were not necessarily lying. They were not making it up. But then neither was Neil Tyson when he talked about Bush's stars speech. When the witnesses said they remembered seeing the suspect at the scene of the crime, they were telling the truth. They did *remember* seeing him there, but they didn't actually see him there. These are two quite different things.

This is not to say that eyewitness testimony is worthless; quite the reverse. In certain circumstances it is invaluable in order to secure convictions. Rather, it is to say that memories should be coaxed out of witnesses with sensitivity to the biases that might otherwise contaminate the evidence. The tragedy is that the techniques used by police, until recently, had little of this sophistication.

The practice of "drive-bys," for example, has been used and abused for decades: this is where an eyewitness is taken by police to see a suspect on the street, or at their place of work. Given that the witness knows that the police have suspicions about the person—why else would they be going there?—the technique is dangerously suggestive.

And one obvious problem is that once a person has viewed the suspect they are liable to transpose his face onto that of the real criminal. Each time they recall the crime scene, they will become more certain that the suspect was really there. A tentative identification is rapidly transformed into cast-iron certainty. As Donald Thomson, a psychologist in Melbourne, put it: "Two months down the track, they go into the witness box and say they are absolutely sure."

Lineups—where a suspect and a number of fillers are placed side by side in a room—are more reliable than drive-bys, but these, too, have been open to abuse. Often they are conducted by an officer who already knows the identity of the suspect, opening up the possibility that he might inadvertently influence the selection with verbal and nonverbal cues. In other cases lineups have been conducted where only one person, the suspect, matches the description.*

And so it goes on. There were so many error traps in the methods used by police that entire book chapters have been written about them. If miscarriages of justice had been investigated, these latent problems would have been discovered, and could have been addressed. Instead, these procedures were used, with only minor variations, for decades.

This was not just bad for suspects, but also for the police, prosecutors, and the public. After all, mistaken identifications cause police to ignore other leads. This often allows the real criminal to roam the streets, perpetrating more crimes.

The Innocence Project has campaigned for a number of reforms. It argues that lineups should always be administered by an officer who doesn't know the identity of the suspect. It also calls for sequential lineups, where suspects and fillers are shown one at a time rather than simultaneously.

When these procedures have been tested, they have significantly reduced mistaken identifications *without compromising accurate identifications*. A field study in 2011, for example, found that "double-blind sequential lineups as administered by police departments across the country resulted in the same number of suspect identifications but fewer known-innocent filler identifications than double blind simultaneous lineups."[11]

Some have disputed these findings and have proposed more tests. But this, in itself, represents progress. Systems are being trialed. People are using experiments. As of 2014, three states are using double-blind sequential administration, and six others have recommended them. This is what an open loop looks like.

A second error trap identified by the Innocence Project is false confessions, which contributed to 30 percent of wrongful convictions.[12] These are often secured from vulnerable people, who are tricked or intimidated into confessing to crimes they didn't commit. Juan Rivera, you will remember, was a vulnerable young man with a history of psychological problems who confessed after days of interrogation. Police experts said he had experienced a psychotic episode.

One reform that could help to eliminate false confessions would be to make the videotaping of interrogations compulsory. This would undermine any incentive to bully or mislead suspects into confessions.

Some police forces worry that such a change might impede their ability to secure confessions from people who are actually guilty. If true, this would count against reform. But a comprehensive review by the Department of Justice found that police departments that had voluntarily taped interviews had not compromised their capacity to secure genuine confessions. As a district attorney in Minnesota put it: "During the past eight years it has become clear that videotaped interrogations have strengthened the ability of police and prosecutors to secure convictions against the guilty."[13]

Another area requiring major reform is forensic science. Some of these techniques, such as hair microscopy, have limited scientific legitimacy. In one murder case, experts "matched" seventeen hairs found at a crime scene with the hair taken from a suspect. He was subsequently convicted. But later testing using hard DNA evidence demonstrated that all seventeen hairs had been misidentified. A pubic hair matched to a male suspect actually belonged to the female victim.[14]

It turns out that hair matching is highly subjective. In 2013 the FBI admitted that in more than two thousand cases between 1985 and 2000, analysts may have exaggerated the significance of hair analysis or reported them inaccurately.[15] The National Academy of Science has said that hair matching is "unreliable."[16] It was this error trap that condemned Jimmy Ray Bromgard, mentioned in chapter 4, to fifteen years in prison for a crime he didn't commit.

And so it goes on. In case after case the Innocence Project discovered predictable pathways to failure; weaknesses that should have been identified and addressed. Other signatures of wrongful conviction include government misconduct, bad advice by lawyers, the use of prison informants (often offered undisclosed incentives to testify against the suspect) and scientific fraud.

Barry Scheck has suggested reform in each of these areas. But perhaps the most significant reform he has called for is the establishment of Criminal Justice Reform Commissions. These are independent bodies mandated to investigate wrongful convictions and to recommend reforms, along the lines of air-accident investigation teams. As of publication, only eleven states had such commissions.

In the UK a Reform Commission of sorts was set up in 1995 following a series of spectacular miscarriages of justice, including the Birmingham Six and the Guildford Four. The Criminal Cases Review Commission, an independent body, has the authority to refer questionable verdicts to the Court of Appeal. Between 1997 and the end of October 2013 the commission referred a total of 538 cases.

Of these, 70 percent succeeded at appeal.

• • •

There is an intriguing coda to the Tyson-Bush episode, as Christopher Chabris and Daniel Simons, two psychologists, point out in an essay for the *New York Times*.[17] For it turns out that George W. Bush was wrong about his memories of 9/11, too.

The former president has often claimed that he saw the first plane crashing into the north tower before going into a classroom in Florida. But he didn't. There was no live footage of a plane hitting the tower so he couldn't have seen it before going into the classroom. As Chabris puts it: "Mr. Bush must have combined information he acquired later with the traces left by his actual experience to produce a new version of events, just as Dr. Tyson did."

This faulty recollection from Bush also had another effect. People assumed that if he saw footage of the crash before going into the classroom, he must have known about the attacks in advance. Had he also been involved in planning them? people asked. This is the stuff of a now-familiar conspiracy theory. But, in fact, there was no conspiracy. It is just that presidents misremember as well.

III

I n our discussion of the criminal justice system, we have largely focused on wrongful convictions. But this shouldn't obscure equally pressing issues. Methods of detection need to be improved to bring unsolved crimes to trial. There is also vital work that needs to be undertaken to reduce the rate at which guilty people walk free. These are tragedies, too, because victims are denied justice and the deterrent effect of the system is undermined.

There is also the problem of the large number of trials where innocent defendants are put in the dock. The data suggest that the acquittal rate is high. That is often hailed as evidence that the justice system is rigorously acquitting the innocent, but it could also mean that millions of pounds are being wasted on unnecessary trials, with the real culprit still at large.

The key issue in all of this, however, is not to allow the perceived trade-offs between these objectives to obscure the deeper fact that progress can be made on each of them *at the same time*. That was the point about wrongful convictions: reforms wouldn't blunt the teeth of the justice system; on the contrary, reforms would, in many cases, make them sharper.

There are also other deep-lying problems, features so integral to the fabric of the system that they tend to go unquestioned. Trial by jury, for example, is often held up as sacrosanct, and it may be the most effective form of deliberation in criminal cases. But shouldn't it be tested? If juries are coming to the wrong conclusions in predictable ways, doesn't it make sense that procedures should be reformed so that these latent problems are addressed?

To see how, consider an experiment not on juries, but on judges. Over a ten-month period, Shai Danziger, a neuroscientist at Tel Aviv University, and colleagues analyzed the parole decisions of eight Israeli judges.[18] Every day each judge considered between fourteen and thirty-five real-life cases, spending around six minutes on each decision. The verdicts represented 40 percent of the parole decisions made in Israel over the ten-month period. Each judge had an average of twenty-two years of experience.

Now, judges are supposed to be rational and deliberative. They are supposed to make decisions on hard evidence. But Danziger found something quite different: if the case was assessed by a judge just after he had eaten breakfast, the prisoner had a 65 percent chance of getting parole. But as time passed through the morning, and the judges got hungry, the chances of parole *gradually diminished to zero*. Only after the judges had taken a break to eat did the odds shoot back up to 65 percent, only to decrease back to 0 over the course of the afternoon.

The judges were oblivious to this astonishing bias in their deliberations. Criminologists and social workers were also unaware of it. Why? Because it had never been analyzed. As one of the co-authors of the study put it: "There are no checks about the judges' decisions because no one has ever documented this tendency before. Needless to say, I would expect there to be something put into place after this."[19]

With regard to juries, things are even worse. It is illegal in the UK to even conduct a study on how juries go about their deliberations. The unstated rationale for this prohibition is that if the public find out how juries operate, they might lose confidence in the system. It is an "ignorance is bliss" approach. But this is as intellectually fraudulent as removing the black box from an airplane to insure that people won't ever find out about pilot error. The result is inevitable: the same mistakes will be made, over and over.

None of this is to argue that the jury system should be abolished. Many juries do brilliant work under stressful circumstances. It is merely to highlight the almost total lack of evidence as to whether juries are working effectively compared with possible alternatives.[*] We cannot sustain this approach indefinitely because miscarriages of justice and other high profile mistakes are corroding trust in the system. Criminal justice, like so many other areas of public life, needs to undergo a high-performance revolution based on something that has historically proved almost impossible: learning from mistakes.

More than twenty years after Juan Rivera was sentenced to life imprisonment for the murder of eleven-year-old Holly Staker, a DNA test was conducted on a blood-stained piece of timber that had been used in a different murder. A man named Delwin Foxworth, who also lived in Lake County, had been savagely beaten with the two-by-four, doused with gasoline, and set on fire. He later died of his injuries having suffered burns over 80 percent of his body.[20]

The murderer was never found, but the DNA test was conclusive. The DNA of the blood found on the two-by-four matched that of the semen found in Holly Staker. Police are now almost certain that the man who got away with the rape and murder of an innocent eleven-year-old back in 1992 went on to commit another murder eight years later. Therefore Foxworth may be yet another victim of the wrongful conviction of Juan Rivera—it allowed the real culprit to get away with it and kill again.

"When we think about miscarriages of justice, we often focus on the person who has been jailed for a crime he didn't commit," Steve Art, a New York lawyer, said.[21] "But there are other consequences, too. When you convict the wrong person, the real criminal is left to roam the streets, committing crimes with sometimes devastating effects. It is yet another reason why we need to learn the lessons."

As for Rivera, he was finally released on January 6, 2012. "I can't explain it. It's life all over again," he said as he walked free. "I just want to experience life. Watch a football game. Just walk on the sidewalk and know that I'm free." Somebody in the crowd handed him a slice of pizza, which he carried with some embarrassment to a car that had been arranged by supporters.

His friends have rallied around, but he will never get back the nineteen years he spent in prison. "I would be lying if I said that I have come to terms with what I went through," he told me. "Even now, I am uneasy and nervous. I can't sleep at night. I can't go into crowded supermarkets. When I am walking down the road, I keep looking around. Nineteen years in prison for a crime you didn't commit leaves a mark."

But what about those who were responsible for sending him to jail? How do they feel about it today? Perhaps it should come as no surprise that even now many remain convinced of Rivera's guilt. In October 2014, Charles Fagan, an investigator who helped obtain Rivera's confessions, was asked by the *Chicago Tribune* if he still believed that Rivera committed the murder. "I think so," he said.[22]

And what of the prosecutors? Even after Rivera was released, some Lake County lawyers wanted to put him back on trial. Only with a further conviction would they be able to say that they had been right all along. Only with a conviction could they quell their dissonance. Rivera walking around free was like an accusation against their competence.

It was left to the Illinois Appellate Court to take what might otherwise seem to be an astonishing step: it barred Lake County from ever prosecuting Juan Rivera for the murder of Holly Staker again.

Part III
CONFRONTING COMPLEXITY

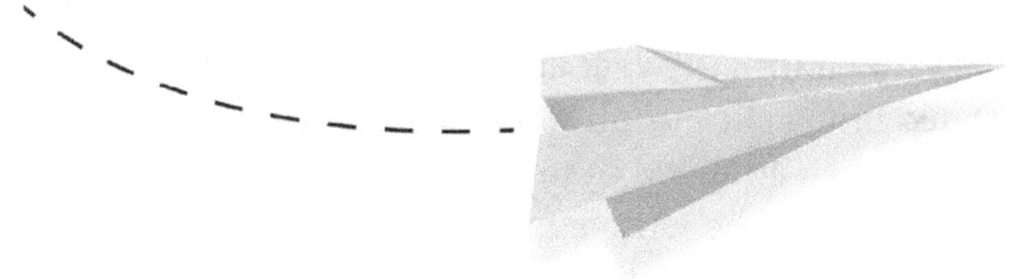

Chapter 7

The Nozzle Paradox

I

U nilever had a problem. They were manufacturing detergent at their factory near Liverpool, in the northwest of England, in the usual way—indeed, the way detergent is still made today. Boiling hot chemicals are forced through a nozzle at super-high levels of pressure and speed out of the other side; as the pressure drops they disperse into vapor and powder.

The vapor is siphoned away while the powder is collected in a vat, where collagen and various other ingredients are added. Then it is packed into boxes, branded with names like Daz and Bold, and sold at a hefty markup. It is a neat business concept, and has become a huge industry. Annual sales of detergent are over $3 billion in the United States alone.

But the problem for Unilever was that the nozzles didn't work smoothly. To quote Steve Jones, who briefly worked at the Liverpool soap factory in the 1970s before going on to become one of the world's most influential evolutionary biologists, they kept clogging up.[1] "The nozzles were a damn nuisance," he has said. "They were inefficient, kept blocking and made detergent grains of different sizes."

This was a major problem for the company, not just because of maintenance and lost time, but also in terms of the quality of the product. They needed to come up with a superior nozzle. Fast.

And so they turned to their crack team of mathematicians. Unilever, even back then, was a rich company, so it could afford the brightest and best. These were not just ordinary mathematicians, but experts in high-pressure systems, fluid dynamics, and other aspects of chemical analysis. They had special grounding in the physics of "phase transition": the processes governing the transformation of matter from one state (liquid) to another (gas or solid).

These mathematicians were what we today might call "intelligent designers." These are the kind of people we generally turn to when we need to solve problems, whether business, technical, or political: get the right people, with the right training, to come up with the optimal plan.

They delved ever deeper into the problems of phase transition, and derived sophisticated equations. They held meetings and seminars. And, after a long period of study, they came up with a new design.

You have probably guessed what is coming: it didn't work. It kept blocking. The powder granularity remained inconsistent. It was inefficient.

Almost in desperation, Unilever turned to its team of biologists. These people had little understanding of fluid dynamics. They would not have known a phase transition if it had jumped up and bitten them. But they had something more valuable: a profound understanding of the relationship between failure and success.

They took ten copies of the nozzle and applied small changes to each one, and then subjected them to failure by testing them. "Some nozzles were longer, some shorter, some had a bigger or smaller hole, maybe a few grooves on the inside," Jones says. "But one of them improved a very small amount on the original, perhaps by just one or two percent."

They then took the "winning" nozzle and created ten slightly different copies, and repeated the process. They then repeated it again, and again. After 45 generations and 449 'failures,' they had a nozzle that was outstanding. It worked "many times better than the original."

Progress had been delivered not through a beautifully constructed master plan (*there was no plan*), but by rapid interaction with the world. A single, outstanding nozzle was discovered as a consequence of testing, and discarding, 449 failures.

II

So far in the book, we have seen that learning from mistakes relies on two components: first, you need to have the right kind of system—one that harnesses errors as a means of driving progress; and second, you need a mindset that enables such a system to flourish.

In the previous section we concerned ourselves with the mindset aspect of this equation. Cognitive dissonance occurs when mistakes are too threatening to admit to, so they are reframed or ignored. This can be thought of as the internal fear of failure: how we struggle to admit mistakes to ourselves.

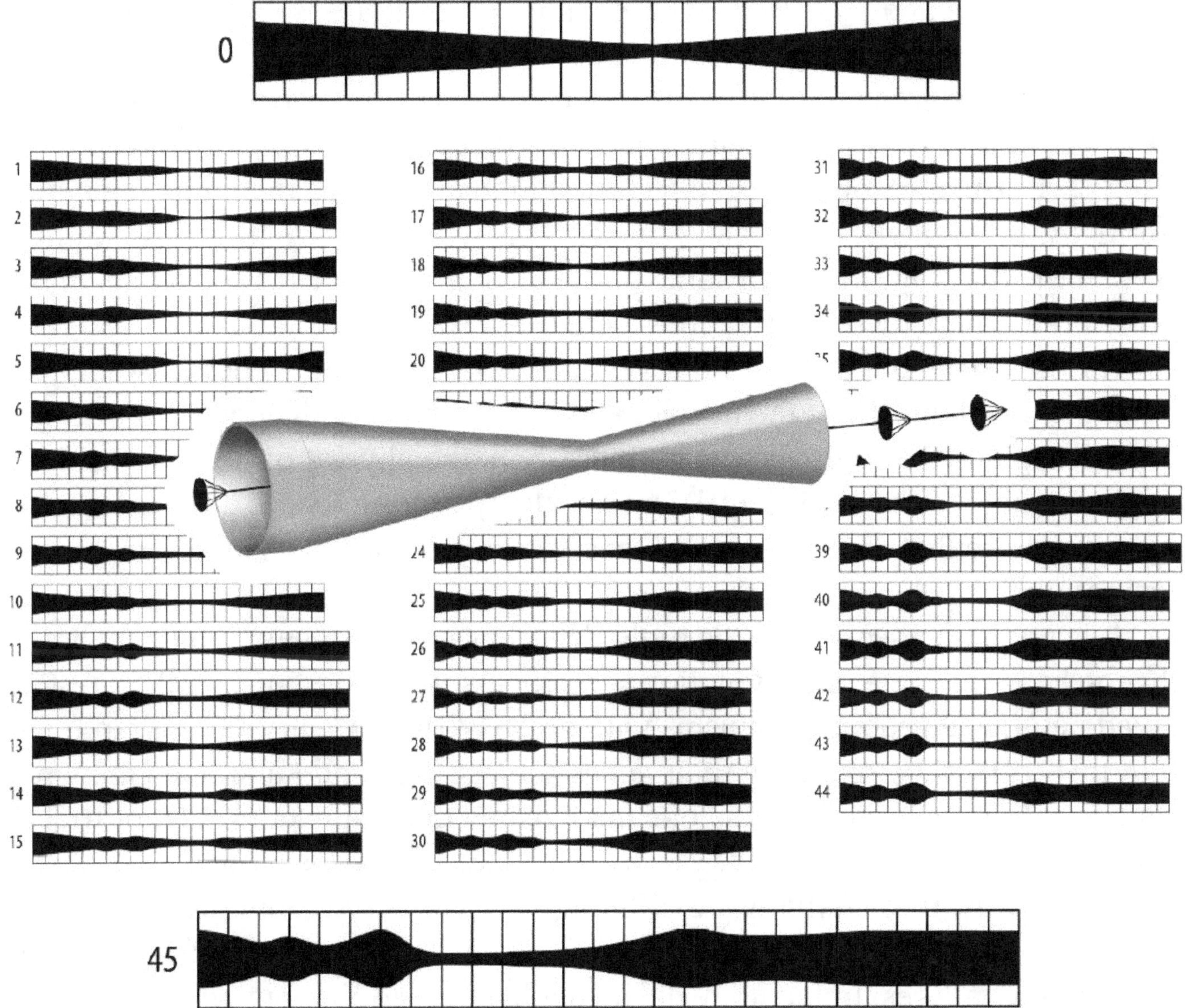

The original nozzle is at the top. The final nozzle, after 45 generations and 449 iterations, is at the bottom. It has a shape no mathematician could possibly have anticipated.

In sections 5 and 6, we will return to this crucial issue. We will look at how to create a culture where mistakes are not reframed or suppressed, but wielded as a means of driving progress. We will also look at the external fear of failure—the fear of being unfairly blamed or punished—which also undermines learning from mistakes.

Ultimately, we will see that strong, resilient, growth-orientated cultures are built from specific psychological foundations, and we will look at practical examples of cutting-edge companies, sports teams, and even schools that are leading the way.

But now we are going to delve into the system side of the equation. We have already touched upon this in our examination of institutions that successfully learn from mistakes, such as aviation and the Virginia Mason Health System. But now we are going to look at the rich theoretical framework that underpins these examples. We will see that *all* systems that learn from failure have a distinctive structure, one that can be found in many places, including the natural world, artificial intelligence, and science. This will then give us an opportunity to examine the ways in which some of the most innovative organizations in the world are harnessing this structure—with often startling results.

It is this structure that is so marvelously evoked by the Unilever example. What the development of the nozzle reveals, above all, is the power of testing. Even though the biologists knew nothing about the physics of phase transition, they were able to develop an efficient nozzle by trialing lots of different ones, rejecting those that didn't work and then varying the best nozzle in each generation.

It is not coincidental that the biologists chose this strategy: it mirrors how change happens in nature. Evolution is a process that relies on a "failure test" called natural selection. Organisms with greater "fitness" survive and reproduce, with their offspring inheriting their genes subject to a random process known as mutation. It is a system, like the one that created the Unilever nozzle, of trial and error.

In one way, these failures are different from those we examined in aviation, health care, and the criminal justice system. The biologists realized they would create many failures: in fact they did so deliberately to find out which designs worked and which didn't. In aviation nobody sets out to fail deliberately. The whole idea is to minimize accidents.

But despite this difference there is a vital similarity. Failures in aviation set the stage for reform. The errors are part and parcel of the dynamic process of change: not just real accidents and failures, but also those that occur in simulators and near-miss events. Likewise, the rejected nozzles helped to drive the progression of the design. They all share an essential pattern: an adaptive process driven by the detection and response to failure.

Evolution as a process is powerful because of its *cumulative* nature. Richard Dawkins offers a neat way to think about cumulative selection in his wonderful book *The Blind Watchmaker*. He invites us to consider a monkey trying to type a single line from *Hamlet*: "Methinks it is like a weasel." The odds are pretty low for the monkey to get it right.

If the monkey is typing at random and there are 27 letters (counting the space bar as a letter), it has a 1 in 27 chance to get the first letter right, a 1 in 27 for the next letter, and so on. So just to get the first three in a row correct are 1/27 multiplied by 1/27 multiplied by 1/27. That is one chance in 19,683. To get all 28 in the sequence, the odds are around 1 in 10,000 million, million, million, million, million, million.

But now suppose that we provide a selection mechanism (i.e., a failure test) that is cumulative. Dawkins set up a computer program to do just this. Its first few attempts at getting the phrase is random, just like a monkey. But then the computer scans the various nonsense phrases to see which is closest, however slightly, to the target phrase. It rejects all the others. It then randomly varies the winning phrase, and then scans the new generation. And so on.

The winning phrase after the first generation of running the experiment on the computer was: WDLTMNLT DTJBSWIRZREZLMQCO P. After ten generations, by honing in on the phrase closest to the target phrase, and rejecting the others, it was: MDLDMNLS ITJISWHRZREZ MECS P. After twenty generations, it looked like this: MELDINLS IT ISWPRKE Z WECSEL. After thirty generations, the resemblance is visible to the naked eye: METHINGS IT ISWLIKE B WECSEL. By the forty-third generation, the computer got the right phrase. It took only a few moments to get there.

Cumulative selection works, then, if there is some form of "memory": i.e., if the results of one selection test are fed into the next, and into the next, and so on. This process is so powerful that, in the natural world, it confers what has been called "the illusion of design": animals that look as if they were designed by a vast intelligence when they were, in fact, created by a blind process.

An echo of this illusion can be seen in the nozzle example. The final shape is so uniquely suited to creating fine-grained detergent that it invites the thought that a master designer must have been at work. In fact, as we have seen, the biologists used no "design" capability at all. They simply harnessed the power of the evolutionary process.

There are many systems in the world that are essentially evolutionary in nature. Indeed, many of the greatest thinkers of the last two centuries favored free market systems because they mimic the process of biological change,[2] as the author Tim Harford notes in his excellent book *Adapt*.[3] Different companies competing with each other, with some failing and some surviving, facilitate the adaptation of the system. This is why markets—provided they are well regulated —are such efficient solvers of problems: they create an ongoing process of trial and error.

The equivalent of natural selection in a market system is bankruptcy. When a company goes bust it is a bit like the failure of a particular nozzle design. It reveals that something (product, price, strategy, advertising, management, process, etc.) wasn't working compared with the competition. Weaker ideas and products are jettisoned. Successful ideas are replicated by other companies. The evolution of the system is driven, just like the design of the Unilever nozzle, by cumulative adaptation.

The failure of companies in a free market, then, is not a defect of the system, or an unfortunate by-product of competition; rather, it is an indispensable aspect of *any* evolutionary process. According to one economist, 10 percent of American companies go bankrupt every year.[4] The economist Joseph Schumpeter called this "creative destruction."

Now, compare this with centrally planned economies, where there are almost no failures at all. Companies are protected from failure by subsidy. The state is protected from failure by the printing press, which can inflate its way out of trouble. At first, this may look like an enlightened way to go about solving the problems of economic production, distribution, and exchange. Nothing ever fails and, by implication, everything looks successful.

But this is precisely why planned economies didn't work. They were manned by intelligent planners who decided how much grain to produce, how much iron to mine, and who used complicated calculations to determine the optimal solutions. But they faced the same problem as the Unilever mathematicians: their ideas, however enlightened, were not tested rapidly enough—and so had little opportunity to be reformed in the light of failure.

Even if the planners were ten times smarter than the businessmen operating in a market economy, they would still fall way behind. Without the benefit of a valid test, the system is plagued by rigidity. In markets, on the other hand, it is the thousands of little failures that lubricate and, in a sense, guide the system. When companies go under, other entrepreneurs learn from these mistakes, the system creates new ideas, and consumers ultimately benefit.

In a roughly similar way, accidents in aviation, while tragic for the passengers on the fatal flights, bolster the safety of future flights. The failure sets the stage for meaningful change.

That is not to say that markets are perfect. There are problems of monopoly, collusion, inequality, price-fixing, and companies that are too big to fail and therefore protected by a taxpayer guarantee. All these things militate against the adaptive process. But the underlying point remains: markets work not in spite of the many business failures that occur, but because of them.

It is not just systems that can benefit from a process of testing and learning; so, too, can organizations. Indeed, many of the most innovative companies in the world are bringing some of the basic lessons of evolutionary theory into the way they think about strategy. Few companies tinker randomly like the Unilever biologists, because with complex problems it can take a long time to home in on a solution.

Rather, they make judicious use of tests, challenge their own assumptions, and wield the lessons to guide strategy. It is a mix of top-down reasoning (as per the mathematicians) and bottom-up iteration (as per the biologists); the fusing of the knowledge they already have with the knowledge that can be gained by revealing its inevitable flaws. It is about having the courage of one's convictions, but also the humility to test early, and to adapt rapidly.

• • •

An echo of these ideas can be seen in the process of technological change. The conventional way we think about technology is that it is essentially top-down in character. Academics conduct high-level research, which creates scientific theories, which are then used by practical people to create machines, gadgets, and other technologies.

This is sometimes called the linear model and it can be represented with a simple flowchart: Research and theory à Technology à Practical applications. In the case of the Industrial Revolution, for example, the conventional picture is that it was largely inspired by the earlier scientific revolution; the ideas of Boyle, Hooke, and Locke gave rise to the machinery that changed the world.

But there is a problem with the linear model: in most areas of human development, it severely underestimates the role of bottom-up testing and learning of the kind adopted by the Unilever biologists. In his book *The Economic Laws of Scientific Research*, Terence Kealey, a practicing scientist, debunks the conventional narrative surrounding the Industrial Revolution:

In 1733, John Kay invented the flying shuttle, which mechanized weaving, and in 1770 James Hargreaves invented the spinning jenny, which as its name implies, mechanized spinning. These major developments in textile technology, as well as those of Wyatt and Paul (spinning frame, 1758), Arkwright (water frame, 1769), presaged the Industrial Revolution, yet they owed nothing to science; they were empirical developments based on the trial, error and experimentation of skilled craftsmen who were trying to improve the productivity, and so the profits, of their factories.[5]

Note the final sentence: these world-changing machines were developed, like Unilever's nozzle, through trial and error. Amateurs and artisans, men of practical wisdom, motivated by practical problems, worked out how to build these machines, by trying, failing, and learning. They didn't fully understand the theory underpinning their inventions. They couldn't have talked through the science. But—like the Unilever biologists—they didn't really need to.[*]

And this is where the direction of causality can flip. Take the first steam engine for pumping water. This was built by Thomas Newcomen, a barely literate, provincial ironmonger and Baptist lay preacher, and developed further by James Watt. The understanding of both men was intuitive and practical. But the success of the engine raised a deep question: *why* does this incredible device actually work (it broke the then laws of physics)? This question inspired Nicolas Léonard Sadi Carnot, a French physicist, to develop the laws of thermodynamics. Trial and error inspired the technology, which in turn inspired the theory. This is the linear model in reverse.

In his seminal book *Antifragile*, Nassim Nicholas Taleb shows how the linear model is wrong (or, at best, misleading) in everything from cybernetics, to derivatives, to medicine, to the jet engine. In each case history reveals that these innovations emerged as a consequence of a similar process utilized by the biologists at Unilever, and became encoded in heuristics (rules of thumb) and practical know-how. The problems were often too complex to solve theoretically, or via a blueprint, or in the seminar room. They were solved by failing, learning, and failing again.

Architecture is a particularly interesting case, because it is widely believed that ancient buildings and cathedrals, with their wonderful shapes and curves, were inspired by the formal geometry of Euclid. How else could the ancients have built these intricate structures? In fact, geometry played almost no role. As

Taleb shows, it is almost certain that the practical wisdom of architects inspired Euclid to write his Book of Elements, so as to formalize what the builders already knew.

"Take a look at Vitruvius' manual, *De architectura*, the bible of architects, written about three hundred years after Euclid's Elements," Taleb writes. "There is little formal geometry in it, and, of course, no mention of Euclid, mostly heuristics, the kind of knowledge that comes out of a master guiding his apprentices . . . Builders could figure out the resistance of materials without the equations we have today—buildings that are, for the most part, still standing."[6]

These examples do not show that theoretical knowledge is worthless. Quite the reverse. A conceptual framework is vital even for the most practical men going about their business. In many circumstances, new theories have led to direct technological breakthroughs (such as the atom bomb emerging from the Theory of Relativity).

The real issue here is speed. Theoretical change is itself driven by a feedback mechanism, as we noted in chapter 3: science learns from failure. But when a theory fails, like say when the Unilever mathematicians failed in their attempt to create an efficient nozzle design, it takes time to come up with a new, all-encompassing theory. To gain practical knowledge, however, you just need to try a different-sized aperture. Tinkering, tweaking, learning from practical mistakes: all have speed on their side. Theoretical leaps, while prodigious, are far less frequent.

Ultimately, technological progress is a complex interplay between theoretical and practical knowledge, each informing the other in an upward spiral*. But we often neglect the messy, iterative, bottom-up aspect of this change because it is easy to regard the world, so to speak, in a top-down way. We try to comprehend it from above rather than discovering it from below.

You can even see the basic contours of this perspective in the modern history of artificial intelligence. When the chess grand-master Garry Kasparov was defeated by Deep Blue in the famous "victory of the machine" match in 1997, it created a storm. The popular interpretation was "computers are better than humans!"

In fact, the real surprise was that Kasparov came so close. Humans can only search three or so moves per second. Deep Blue could search two hundred million moves per second. It was designed to look deep into the various possibilities. But, crucially, it could not search every possibility due to the vast number of permutations (chess is characterized by a certain kind of complexity).

Moreover, although it had been preprogrammed with a great deal of chess knowledge, it couldn't learn from its own mistakes as it played the games.

This gave Kasparov a fighting chance, because he had something the computer largely lacked: practical knowledge developed through trial and error. He could look at the configuration of pieces on a board, recognize its meaning based upon long experience, and then instantly select moves. It was this practical knowledge which almost propelled him to victory despite a formidable computational deficit. Deep Blue won the series three and a half to two and a half.

But artificial intelligence has moved on since then.[7] One of the vogue ideas is called *temporal difference learning*. When designers created TD-Gammon, a program to play backgammon, they did not provide it with any preprogrammed chess knowledge or capacity to conduct deep searches. Instead, it made moves, predicted what would happen next, and then looked at how far its expectations were wide of the mark. That enabled it to update its expectations, which it took into the next game.

In effect, TD-Gammon was a trial-and-error program. It was left to play day and night against itself, developing practical knowledge. When it was let loose on human opponents, it defeated the best in the world. The software that enabled it to learn from error was sophisticated, but its main strength was that it didn't need to sleep, so could practice all the time.

In other words it had the opportunity to fail more often.

III

Before we go on to look at what all this means in practice, and how we might harness the evolutionary process in organizations and in our lives, let us deal with a question that immediately arises: isn't it just *obvious* that we should test our assumptions if there is a cost-effective way of doing so? Why would any business leader, politician, or, indeed, sports team do otherwise?

It turns out, however, that there is a profound obstacle to testing, a barrier that prevents many of us from harnessing the upsides of the evolutionary process. It can be summarized simply, although the ramifications are surprisingly deep: we are hardwired to think that the world is simpler than it really is. And if the world is simple, why bother to conduct tests? If we already have the answers, why would we feel inclined to challenge them?

This tendency to underestimate the complexity around us is now a well-studied aspect of human psychology and it is underpinned, in part, by the so-called narrative fallacy. This term was coined by the philosopher Nassim Nicholas Taleb and has been studied by the Nobel Prize–winner Daniel Kahneman: it refers to our propensity to create stories about what we see *after the event.*

You see the narrative fallacy in operation when an economist pops up on the early-evening news and explains why the markets moved in a particular direction during the day. His arguments are often immaculately presented. They are intuitive and easy to follow. But they raise a question: Why, if the market movements are so easy to understand, was he unable to predict the market movement in advance? Why is he generally playing catch-up?

Another example of the narrative fallacy comes from sports punditry. In December 2007, Fabio Capello, an Italian, became head coach of the England soccer team. He was a disciplinarian. He ordered players to arrive at meetings five minutes early, clamped down on cell phones, and even banned tomato ketchup in the cafeteria. These actions were highly visible and well reported. This is what psychologists call "salience." And the results on the pitch were, at the outset, very good.

Rather like the economists on the early evening news, soccer journalists began to tell a simple and convincing story as to why the team was doing well: it was about Capello's authoritarian manner. His methods were eulogized. Finally, a coach who was willing to give the players a kick up the rear! At last, a coach who has provided discipline to those slackers! One flattering headline read: "The Boss!"

But at the FIFA World Cup, the biggest competition in the sport, England bombed. They limped through the qualifying stage before being decisively eliminated with a 4–1 defeat by Germany. Almost instantly the narrative flipped. Capello is too tough! He is taking the fun out of the game! The Italian is treating our players like children! Many soccer journalists didn't even notice that they had attempted to explain contradictory effects with the same underlying cause.

That is the power of the narrative fallacy. We are so eager to impose patterns upon what we see, so hardwired to provide explanations that we are capable of "explaining" opposite outcomes with the same cause without noticing the inconsistency.

In truth, England's soccer results were not caused not by the salient features of Capello's actions, but by myriad factors that were not, in advance, predictable.

That is why soccer journalists who are brilliant at explaining why teams won or lost after the event are not much better than amateurs at predicting who is going to win or lose beforehand. Daniel Kahneman has said:

> Narrative fallacies arise inevitably from our continuous attempt to make sense of the world. The explanatory stories that people find compelling are simple; are concrete rather than abstract; assign a larger role to talent, stupidity, and intentions than to luck; and focus on a few striking events that happened rather than on the countless events that failed to happen. Any recent salient event is a candidate to become the kernel of a causal narrative.[8]

But think about what this means in practice. If we view the world as simple, we are going to expect to understand it without the need for testing and learning. The narrative fallacy, in effect, biases us toward top-down rather than bottom-up. We are going to trust our hunches, our existing knowledge, and the stories that we tell ourselves about the problems we face, rather than testing our assumptions, seeing their flaws, and learning.

But this tendency, in turn, changes the psychological dynamic of organizations and systems. The greatest difficulty that many people face, as we have seen, is in admitting to their personal failures, and thus learning from them. We have looked at cognitive dissonance, which becomes so severe that we often reframe, spin, and sometimes even edit out our mistakes.

Now think of the Unilever biologists. They didn't regard the rejected nozzles as failures because they were part and parcel of how they learned. All those rejected designs were regarded as central to their strategy of cumulative selection, not as an indictment of their judgment. They knew they would have dozens of failures and were therefore not fazed by them.

But when we are misled into regarding the world as simpler than it really is, we not only resist testing our top-down strategies and assumptions, we also become more defensive when they are challenged by our peers or by the data. After all, if the world is simple, you would have to be pretty stupid not to understand it.

Think back to the divide between aviation and health care. In aviation there is a profound respect for complexity. Pilots and system experts are deeply aware that they are dealing with a world they do not fully understand, and never will.

They regard failures as an inevitable consequence of the mismatch between the complexity of the system and their capacity to understand it.

This reduces the dissonance of mistakes, increases the motivation to test assumptions in simulators and elsewhere, and makes it "safe" for people to speak up when they spot issues of concern. The entire system is about preventing failure, about doing everything possible to stop mistakes happening, but this runs alongside the sense that failures are, in a sense, "normal."

In health care, the assumptions are very different. Failures are seen not as an inevitable consequence of complexity, but as indictments of those who make them, particularly among senior doctors whose self-esteem is bound up with the notion of their infallibility. It is difficult to speak up about concerns, because powerful egos come into play. The consequence is simple: the system doesn't evolve.

Now, let us take these insights into the real world and, in particular, the rapidly-growing industry of high technology.

IV

D rew Houston was getting frustrated. A young computer programmer from Massachusetts, he had a creative idea for a high-tech start-up. It was an online file sharing and storage service, which seamlessly uploads files and replicates them across all computers and devices.

Houston thought of the idea while traveling on a bus from Boston to New York. He opened his laptop but realized he had forgotten his flash drive, which meant that he couldn't do the work he wanted to. "I had a big list of things I wanted to get done. I fished around in my pockets only to find out I'd forgotten my thumb drive," he said. "I was like: 'I never want to have this problem again.'"[9]

He was so annoyed with himself that he started to write some code that would remove the need for a flash drive. Then he realized that this was something everyone could benefit from. "This wasn't a problem unique to me; it was a problem that everyone faced. As a product, it might really sell," he said.

Houston toured venture capital companies but they kept raising the same issue. The market for storage and file sharing was already pretty crowded. Houston explained that these alternative products were rarely used because they were clunky and time-consuming. A more streamlined product would be different, he said. But he couldn't get through.

"It was a challenge to raise our first money because these investors would say: 'There are a hundred of these storage companies. Why does the world need another one of them?' I would respond with: 'Yes, there are a lot of these companies out there, but do you use any of them?' And invariably, they would say: 'Well, no.'"

Houston was clever enough to know that his product wasn't a guaranteed winner. Predicting whether consumers will actually buy a product is often treacherous. But he was quietly confident and wanted to give it a go. However, after a year he wondered if he would ever get a shot. He was close to desperate.

$$\bullet \ \bullet \ \bullet$$

Let us leave Houston for a moment or two and look at two other tech entrepreneurs—Andre Vanier and Mike Slemmer, grappling with a different problem. They had an idea for a free online information service called 1-800-411-SAVE. Unlike Houston they had the money to develop the software. But they had very different ideas about how to write the code, as the author Peter Sims reveals in his book *Little Bets*.[10]

Vanier, a former consultant with McKinsey, thought they should spend plenty of time in the office getting the software absolutely right, so that it was capable of supporting all the millions of users they hoped to attract. He believed that the people at the company had great ability and, given time, would come up with bug-free and efficient software. This is the old perspective on development, with its emphasis on rigorous top-down planning.

Slemmer had a different view. He had already started two tech companies and realized something profound: it is pretty much impossible to come up with perfect code the first time around. It is only when people are using the software, putting it under strain, that you see the bugs and deficiencies you could never have anticipated. By putting the code out there and subjecting it to trial and error you learn the insights that create progress. Why, he asked Vanier, would you try to answer every question before you have a single user?

The debate between Slemmer and Vanier echoes the contrast between the biologists and mathematicians at Unilever (and at a higher level of abstraction between Kealey's idea of progress and those who think progress always emerges from theoretical advance): it is pitting top-down against bottom-up. Vanier wanted to get everything right via a blueprint while Slemmer wanted to test early, and then iterate rapidly while receiving feedback from consumers, thus developing new insights. He wanted to test his assumptions.

Slemmer's arguments won out. The company got the software out at an early stage of development, and rapidly learned the inevitable flaws in their pre-market reasoning. They had to rewrite large sections, learning new insights that increased in direct proportion to the growing user base. Ultimately they developed arguably the most sophisticated software in the industry.

"Although they competed against substantially larger, better-resourced companies . . . they were consistently first to identify new features and services such as driving directions and integrated web-phone promotional offers," Peter Sims, the tech author who followed the company's progress, has written. "As Vanier explains, if he can launch ten features in the same time it takes a competitor to launch one, he'll have ten times the amount of experience to draw from in figuring out what has failed the test of customer acceptance and what has succeeded."[11]

This story hints at the dangers of "perfectionism": of trying to get things right the first time. The story of Rick, a brilliant computer scientist living in Silicon Valley, will highlight the problem even more starkly.

Rick had the idea of creating a Web service that would allow people to post simple text articles online. He had this idea well before the blogging revolution. He could sense the potential and worked on it fifteen hours a day. Soon he had a working prototype. But instead of giving consumers a chance to use it, perceive its weaknesses, and then make changes, he decided the software would run more efficiently if he could design a more sophisticated programming language. He spent the next four years designing this new language. It proved disastrous. Two psychologists, Ryan Babineaux and John Krumboltz, have written:

> Over the next four years, he got more and more mired in technical details and lost sight of his original idea. Meanwhile, other entrepreneurs began to build blogging platforms that were neither perfect nor technologically advanced. The difference was that they quickly put their flawed efforts out into the world for others to try. In doing so, they received crucial feedback, evolved their software, and made millions of dollars.[12]

The desire for perfection rests upon two fallacies. The first resides in the miscalculation that you can create the optimal solution sitting in a bedroom or ivory tower and thinking things through rather than getting out into the real world and testing assumptions, thus finding their flaws. It is the problem of valuing top-down over bottom-up.

The second fallacy is the fear of failure. Earlier on we looked at situations where people fail and then proceed to either ignore or conceal those failures. Perfectionism is, in many ways, more extreme. You spend so much time designing and strategizing that you don't get a chance to fail at all, at least until it is too late. It is *pre-closed loop* behavior. You are so worried about messing up that you never even get on the field of play.

In their book *Art and Fear* David Bayles and Ted Orland tell the story of a ceramics teacher who announced on the opening day of class that he was dividing the students into two groups. Half were told that they would be graded on quantity. On the final day of term, the teacher said he would come to class with some scales and weigh the pots they had made. They would get an "A" for 50 lbs of pots, a "B" for 40 lbs, and so on. The other half would be graded on quality. They just had to bring along their one, perfect pot.

The results were emphatic: the works of highest quality were all produced by the group graded for *quantity*. As Bayles and Orland put it: "It seems that while the 'quantity' group was busily churning out piles of work—and learning from their mistakes—the 'quality' group had sat theorizing about perfection, and in the end had little more to show for their efforts than grandiose theories and a pile of dead clay."[13]

You see this in politics, too. Politicians come up with theories (bordering on ideologies) about whether, say, wearing school uniform improves discipline. They talk to psychologists and debate the issue in high-level meetings. It is an elaborate, top-down waste of time. They end up with dead clay. They should conduct a test, see what works, and what doesn't. They will fail more, but that is precisely why they will learn more.

Babineaux and Krumboltz, the two psychologists, have some advice for those who are prone to the curse of perfectionism. It involves stating the following mantras: "If I want to be a great musician, I must first play a lot of bad music." "If I want to become a great tennis player, I must first lose lots of tennis games." "If I want to become a top commercial architect known for energy-efficient, minimalist designs, I must first design inefficient, clunky buildings."

The notion of getting into the trial and error process early informs one of the most elegant ideas to have emerged from the high-tech revolution: *the lean start-*

up. This approach contains a great deal of jargon, but is based upon a simple insight: the value of testing and adapting. High-tech entrepreneurs are often brilliant theorists. They can perform complex mathematics in their sleep. But the lean start-up approach forces them to fuse these skills with what they can discover from failure.

How does it work? Instead of designing a product from scratch, techies attempt to create a "minimum viable product" or MVP. This is a prototype with sufficient features in common with the proposed final product that it can be tested on early adopters (the kind of consumers who buy products early in the life cycle and who influence other people in the market).

These tests answer two vital questions. The first is the fundamental one of, Will people buy our product? If the MVP sufficiently resembles the proposed final product, but none of the early adopters have any interest in it, then you can be pretty sure that the entire business plan is worth ripping up. You have saved a huge amount of time and money by failing early.

But if the MVP looks like a possible winner, you can now find out how it can be improved further. This is the second question answered by the lean start-up approach. You can see what features the consumers like and what they don't like; you can see flaws in the concept and vary its assumptions as you develop toward the final product. In other words, you have hardwired the evolutionary process into the design of the business.

• • •

And this brings us back to Drew Houston. His problem, you'll remember, was that he couldn't raise the funds to get his file sharing idea off the ground. Investors were not confident his idea would get anywhere.

What's worse, it was almost impossible to create a working prototype. After all, Houston's basic pitch was that the file sharing product would only prove its value if it could seamlessly integrate multiple platforms and operating systems. To do that in even minimal form required a huge amount of work, based on deep knowledge of the various systems.

But Houston had an insight. He realized that the MVP doesn't need to be a working prototype at all. All it has to do is mimic the essential features of the final product. Provided it is sufficiently representative it can demonstrate whether consumers really want to buy it and thus kick-start the process of trial and error.

So Houston created a video that showed how the product would work in practice. There was no software, no code, but he didn't need these for his MVP. After all, how do you decide if you want a piece of software? You often look over the shoulder of someone who has got it, and is raving about it, and watch what it does. That is precisely what Houston did with his video.[14]

Eric Ries, the technology entrepreneur and author, picks up the story:

> The video is banal, a simple three-minute demonstration of the technology as it is meant to work, but it was targeted at a community of early adopters. Drew narrates the video personally, and as he's narrating, the viewer is watching his screen. As he describes the kinds of files he'd like to synchronize, the viewer can watch his mouse manipulate his computer. Of course, if you're paying attention, you start to notice that the files he's moving around are full of in-jokes and humorous references that were appreciated by this community of early adopters.[15]

The effects were breathtaking. "It drove hundreds of thousands of people to the website," Houston has said. "Our beta waiting list went from 5,000 people to 75,000 people literally overnight. It totally blew us away."[16]

Houston had demonstrated that people wanted the product. It enabled him to raise more capital and continue product development with confidence. But it also enabled him to interact with the early adopters, develop practical knowledge, and refine the product. That is the value of the lean start-up.

Nick Swinmurn, another technology entrepreneur, created a rather different MVP. He reckoned the world needed a website in order to purchase a stylish collection of shoes. He could have gone about this in the usual way: raising millions in capital, creating a vast inventory, and developing relationships with all the various manufacturers: i.e., designing the entire company from scratch from a blueprint. In other words, top-down.

Instead, he toured various shops and asked if he could take photos of their shoes. In return for allowing him to take the pictures and posting them online, he said he would come back and purchase the shoes at full price if customers registered their interest. By this process, Swinmurn was able to test the so-called value hypothesis: do customers actually want to buy shoes online? It turned out that they did.

But he discovered a host of other things, too. By interacting with real customers he learned things he could never have imagined in advance. He had to deal with returns, complaints, and taking online payment. "This is decidedly different from market research," Ries writes. "If Swinmurn had relied on existing market research or conducted a survey, it could have asked what customers thought they wanted. By building a product instead, albeit a simple one, the company learned much more."[17]

In 2009 Swinmurn sold his company, Zappos, to Amazon for $1.2 billion.

• • •

Steve Jobs is a man who is often held up for his vision. He wasn't interested in feedback and iteration, he wanted to change the world. We will explore how big, creative leaps happen in chapter 10. But in the meantime it is worth noting that when it came to many of his strategic decisions, Jobs harnessed feedback in often powerful ways.

When he took Apple into retail in the early 2000s, for example, he didn't buy a string of stores and try to make the whole thing fly instantly. Rather, he bought a warehouse and started to test his hunches and convictions, and those of his retail experts. The first approach bombed, as Jim Collins reveals in his book *Great by Choice*. "We were like, 'Oh God, we're screwed!'" Jobs said.

So along with Ron Johnson, his retail leader, he kept redesigning and testing. Eventually they opened two stores in Virginia and Los Angeles, enabling them to test some more. Only when they had learned from direct feedback and early failures did they roll out big, across the nation, with disciplined consistency.[18]

The lean start-up approach has many parallels in the modus operandi of innovative companies. In its early days, 3M, the technology conglomerate, relied on a team of product developers for new ideas. They would brainstorm, think deeply, and then, when they had developed completed products, they would show them to end users to see how they reacted. It seemed like a rational process —but it was too slow.

In the mid-1990s they transformed their approach by bringing early adopters into the design process itself. They asked them to try early prototypes, observed them as they used the products, noticed what they liked and what they didn't. This enabled them to test their assumptions again and again.

3M then compared the two approaches. The results weren't even close. As the author Peter Sims puts it: "A study published in 2002 found that using [the] active user strategy to identify and develop ideas generated an average of $146 million after five years, more than eight times higher than the average project developed using traditional, in-house 3M idea-generation methods."[19]

Many other "failure-based" notions are finding their way into business. Agile scrum development and the fail-fast approach are just two of these. Some are doubtless more effective than others. All would benefit from further testing (systems devoted to trial and error themselves benefit from trial and error). None should be used in the wrong context.

But the key significance of this family of ideas, which have helped to develop many of the world's most innovative products, is that they present a riposte to the historic presumption of top-down over bottom-up.

Drew Houston, the entrepreneur we started with in this section, has learned an important psychological lesson too. To leverage the power of failure, you have to be resilient and open. In other words, you have to have the right mindset as well as the right system. If you run away from mistakes, you won't get anywhere. "It is a very grueling experience," he said. "One day you are on top of the world . . . the next day there is a huge bug and the site is down and you are tearing your hair out . . . And guess what: that is still true today."[20]

In 2014 Houston's company was valued at just over $10 billion. It is called Dropbox.

V

There is a metaphor that neatly summarizes these insights. It comes from David Lane, professor at Henley Business School and a leading thinker on complexity.[21] The problem today, he says, is that we operate with a *ballistic model* of success. The idea is that once you've identified a target (creating a new website, designing a new product, improving a political outcome) you come up with a really clever strategy designed to hit the bull's-eye.

You construct the perfect rifle. You create a model of how the bullet will be affected by wind and gravity. You do your math to get the strategy just right. Then you calibrate the elevation of the rifle, pull the trigger, and watch as the bullet sails toward the target.

This approach is flawed for two reasons. First, the real world contains greater complexity than just wind and gravity: there are endless variables and interdependencies. Take a policy as simple as reducing the dangers of smoking by cutting tar and nicotine in cigarettes. It sounds great in theory, particularly when used in conjunction with a clever marketing campaign. It looks like a ballistic strategy perfectly designed to hit an important public health target. But when this idea was implemented in practice, it failed. Smokers compensated for the lack of nicotine by smoking more cigarettes and taking longer and deeper drags. The net result was an *increase* in carcinogens and carbon monoxide.[22] That is what happens in systems populated by human beings: there are unintended consequences. And this is why it is difficult to formulate an effective strategy from on high, via a blueprint.

The second problem is even more elemental. By the time you have designed the rifle, let alone pulled the trigger, the target will have moved. This is the problem of a rapidly changing world. Just look at how IT products are becoming obsolete even before they roll off the production line. This kind of rapid change is only likely to accelerate.

What to do? Professor Lane recommends an entirely different concept of success: the *guided-missile* approach. Sure, you want to design a great rifle, you want to point it at the target, and you want to come up with a decent model of how it will be affected by the known variables, such as the wind and gravity. But it is also vital to react to what happens *after you pull the trigger*.

As soon as the bullet leaves the muzzle, as soon as it comes into contact with the real world—this is when you start to discover the flaws in the blueprint. You find out that the wind is stronger than you anticipated, that it is raining, and that there are unknown variables, interacting with each other as well as with the bullet, which you couldn't possibly have comprehended in advance.

The key is to adjust the flight of the bullet, to integrate this new information into the ongoing trajectory. Success is not just dependent on *before-the-event reasoning*, it is also about *after-the-trigger adaptation*. The more you can detect failure (i.e., deviation from the target), the more you can finesse the path of the bullet onto the right track. And this, of course, is the story of aviation, of biological evolution and well-functioning markets.

This reasoning illustrates the balance between top-down and bottom-up. If the original ballistic plan is hopeless, if the bullet just dribbles out of the muzzle, precision guidance is not going to help very much. But likewise, if you just rely on a ballistic plan, however sophisticated, you are going to hit thin air. It is by getting the balance right between top-down strategy and a rigorous adaptation process that you hit the target. It is fusing what we already know, and what we can still learn.

In the coming decades, Professor Lane argues, success will not just be about intelligence and talent. These things are important; but they should never overshadow the significance of identifying where one's strategy is going wrong, and evolving.

Systems and organizations that foster the growth of knowledge of all kinds will dominate. This is the insight that the high-tech world has been gravitating toward and that much of the rest of the world, with only a few heroic exceptions, is studiously resisting.

Think about the ratio of Unilever again: 449 failures to create a single success. Has your company failed that often, and been honest enough to admit it? Has your school? Has your government department? If they haven't, you are likely to be off target.

It is pointless getting upset about this. Clinging to cherished ideas because you are personally associated with them is tantamount to ossification. As the great British economist John Maynard Keynes put it: "When my information changes, I alter my conclusions. What do you do, sir?"

VI

To conclude this chapter, let us take one final example that reveals the dangers of trusting narrative above testing and learning. It is from the field of international development and a powerful case study because it reveals that the consequences of relying on top-down intuition can sometimes be measured in lost lives.

Specifically, let us take the scourge of AIDS and HIV in Africa. There are a number of alternative approaches to preventing and treating this disease that, on the face of it, seem highly plausible. All of them look like positive ways to alleviate a pressing (and often lethal) problem. But which is the most effective? What does top-down judgment tell you?

> Option 1: surgical treatment for Kaposi's sarcoma, an AIDS defining illness

> Option 2: antiretroviral therapy to combat the virus in infected people

Option 3: prevention of transmission from mother to baby during pregnancy

Option 4: condom distribution to prevent general transmission

Option 5: education for high-risk groups like sex workers

They all sound pretty good, don't they? You can imagine that each approach has its own charity with its own website, glossy material, testimonies from people who have personally benefited from the program, and promotional video. This is how most charities operate. And, on this basis, you would probably invest your money with the organization with the most convincing narrative. In the absence of data, narrative is the best we have.

But this is why we need to conduct tests, to challenge our hunches, and the narrative fallacies upon which they are often based. And when proper trials have been conducted, it turns out that these different programs, which all look so impressive, have vastly different outcomes. It is not just that some of the approaches are a couple of times better; or five times better; or even ten times. The best of the options listed above is *1,400 times as cost-effective* as the worst option.[23]

On the graph below, the treatment for Kaposi's sarcoma doesn't even register.

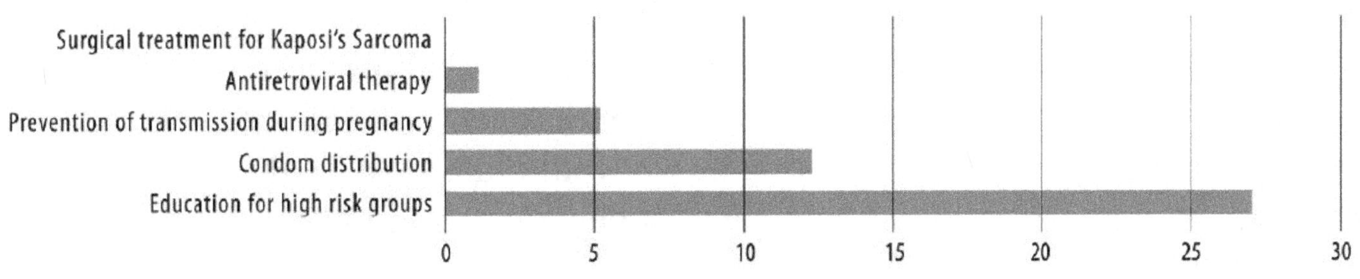

It is for this reason that many of the most influential development campaigners argue that the most important issue when it comes to charitable giving is not just raising more money, but conducting tests, understanding what is working and what isn't, and learning. Instead of trusting in narrative, we should be wielding the power of the evolutionary mechanism.

"Ignoring effectiveness does not mean losing 10% or 20% of the potential value that a health budget could have achieved, but can easily mean losing 99%

or more," Toby Ord, a philosopher at Oxford University, has said. "In practical terms, this can mean hundreds or thousands or millions of additional deaths due to a failure to prioritize. In non-life-saving contexts, it means thousands or millions of people with untreated disabling conditions."[24]

The problem is not just that the donors don't know the effectiveness of rival approaches; neither do many of the charities. The power of the narrative fallacy, the stories of the lives being saved, and the testimonies told by people who have benefited are as convincing to people running charities as to those donating to them. Indeed, why would you wish to collect data when you can meet and talk to those whose lives have been saved?

But given that there may be an alternative treatment that can save more lives, benefit more people—sometimes hundreds or even thousands more—our faith in the evidence of our own eyes is often insufficient. It is by testing that we gain access to the feedback that drives progress, and, in the case of charities, saves lives.

One of the ironies of charitable spending is that the one statistic many donors *do* tend to look at can actually undermine the pursuit of evidence. The so-called overhead ratio measures the amount of money spent on administration compared with the front line. Most donors are keen for charities to keep this ratio low: they want money to go to those who really need it rather than office staff.

But given that evidence-gathering counts as an administrative cost rather than treatment, this makes it even more difficult for charities to conduct tests. As Ord puts it: "You might think that organizations would know the most effective treatment. But often they don't and one of the reasons for that is because they don't do as much program evaluation as we would like because they're trying to keep the overhead ratio low. Also, they just generally aren't aware of these figures."[25]

Ord has set up an organization that encourages people to give 10 percent of their lifetime income to charity, but only to those projects with a proven track record of success.[26] "Our intuitions about what works are often wrong," he says. "We have to test and learn if we are serious about saving lives and alleviating suffering."

Chapter 8

Scared Straight?

I

On a cool morning in the spring of 1978, seventeen teenagers from New Jersey and New York were driven to Rahway State Prison, one of the most notorious detention centers in North America. As they walked up the gravel path to the forbidding set of buildings, the youngsters joked and giggled. They were cocky, had lots of swagger.

The kids—fourteen boys, three girls, of different ethnic groups, aged between fifteen and seventeen—had one thing in common: all had been in trouble with the law. Terence, a seventeen-year-old African American, had stolen cars. Lori, a pretty white sixteen-year-old with a wide smile and large earrings, was a thief and a drug dealer. Angelo, a teenager with unkempt hair and a wispy mustache, had robbed shops in his neighborhood.[1]

Nearly half of all serious crime in America was, at the time, committed by children between ten and seventeen. Arrests for burglary were reportedly 54 percent juvenile; those for car theft were 53 percent juvenile.[2] Rape had been on the rise. These seventeen kids, still joking as they reached the gates of the prison, were not just an isolated group of delinquents, they were symbolic of a wider social problem facing the United States.

Their visit to Rahway was part of a crime-reduction program called "Scared Straight." The idea was that by giving these youngsters a glimpse of prison life —what it is really like inside a maximum security installation—they would be shocked, or at least nudged, into a change of behavior. The program, which had been conceived by the inmates, had been running for two years.

The kids didn't buy the premise, of course. Nobody was going to frighten them out of stealing and mugging. They were too tough to be intimidated by anyone, least of all the jailbirds at Rahway. "They don't scare me," one of the youngsters said with a shrug of the shoulders. "I think it's going to be great going in and seeing all them burnouts," Lori said, laughing.

As they walked through the metal detector at the entrance of the prison, however, the youngsters experienced a first tremor of apprehension. "Line up against the wall!" a sergeant shouted. "You may think this is a sightseeing trip. It isn't. When you went through the door, the man who brought you lost jurisdiction over you. You're in our hands. You'll do as we say. The first thing is to stop smoking! And don't chew gum! And take off those hats!"

This was not what they were expecting. They were ordered to walk in single file into the main prison area as an iron door slammed behind them. They were now in the bowels of a maximum security prison. Up on the balcony convicted prisoners looked down on them. "There's a sweet mother****** right there, with the yellow shirt on!" a muscular black convict yelled. "When you are here, you'll be my bitch," another said menacingly. The kids looked at the guards for a reaction, but there was no response. Their fear heightened.

They were then walked through a cell block called "the hole," populated by prisoners in solitary confinement. The sexual jibes at this stage are too shocking to report. The kids became ever more uncertain. The swagger had vanished. You could see the confusion and fear on their faces. But they were not even thirty minutes into their initiation.

For the next two hours, they were locked in a small room with twenty lifers: prisoners who have been given minimum sentences of twenty-five years. Together, their terms added up to nearly a thousand years. This is where the intervention really began. One at a time, the lifers stood up and offered an insight into what the youngsters could expect if they ever came to Rahway.

"Two of you guys I don't like," a convict with a life sentence for murder screamed at the kids. "I don't like you and I don't like you. You got one time to smile at me and I am going to turn your teeth upside down. You understand? I have just got out of the hole today and I am going to turn your teeth upside down."

The kids had arrived at Rahway with the vague idea that prison was an easy ride. They thought they could just breeze through. They thought they were tough. As they listened, they were systematically disabused of their naïveté. Another inmate asked:

> When we got sexual desires, who do you think we get? Take a wild
> guess . . . We get young, dumb mother*******, just like you. I am in

here ten years and I am going to die in this stinking joint. And if they want to give me these three bitches right here I would leap over them like a kangaroo just to get to one young, pretty . . .

One day you are lying on your blanket, and your mind is drifting over those thirty foot walls and you are thinking about who's with your girl when three guys will slide into your cell, wrap you up in that blanket, and I don't care how tough you think you are or how strong you might be, but they are going to kick you onto the side of that bed, and they are going to [rape you].

None of the kids were talking now. One or two were crying. The lifers were not acting out of spite. They were, in effect, issuing warnings, admonishing the kids to change before it was too late. This was an attempt to deter the next generation of criminals. The lifers didn't want the youngsters to make the same mistakes they had.

"We don't get paid for doing this," the kids were told. "We don't get no extra reward, no extra benefits, no nothing. We do it because we *want* to do it. Because we might help you." Another convict said: "I have been here seven years. I regret every day I have been here . . . You have the best opportunity in the world [to avoid prison] . . . You would have to be a fucking fool not to take it."

The kids were inside Rahway for three hours, but it seemed like three days. They had seen the reality of prison and were adamant they would never go back. Crime no longer seemed cool, but a game that led to hopelessness and desperation. On the way home they were silent. At one point the driver had to stop the car so that one of the boys could vomit.

"I was just so scared, I don't want to go to one of them things," Lori, the girl with the big earrings, said. "It scared the shit out of me, I didn't like it at all."

"I think it will change my life," another said, wide-eyed. "I mean I have got to cut some of this [crime] out. All of it, if possible . . . I am going to try very hard." Others talked about going to college: anything to avoid jail.

The prison visit was recorded by Arnold Shapiro, a documentary maker. His film of the visit was later broadcast by KTLA, Channel 5 in Los Angeles and fronted by Peter Falk of *Columbo* fame. Viewers were riveted by the grim reality of prison life and by the seemingly incredible results of the Scared Straight program. Falk revealed that of the seventeen youngsters, sixteen were still going straight three months later. He also reported that the wider program had had a dramatic impact on reoffending rates. Falk said:

> Over 8,000 juvenile delinquents have sat in fear on these hard wooden benches and for the first time they really heard the brutal reality of crime and prison. The results of this unique program are astounding. Participating communities report that 80 to 90 percent of the kids that they send to Rahway go straight after leaving this stage. That is an amazing success story. And it is unequalled by traditional rehabilitation methods.

Politicians lined up to praise the program. Newspaper columns were penned. Social commentators praised the approach of Scared Straight. Feckless kids were pushed into line and brought face-to-face with the consequences of their actions. It was the kind of short, sharp shock treatment that pundits had been crying out for. It was razor-edged deterrence.[3]

During the week of March 5, 1979, Shapiro's documentary was shown in two hundred major cities.[4] The following month it won the Oscar for best documentary feature at the Academy Awards. The Scared Straight program was rolled out across the United States, Canada, the UK, Australia, and Norway. Its effectiveness was attested to by judges, correction officers, and other experts.

The data seemed remarkable. As George Nicola, a juvenile judge who worked in New Brunswick, a few miles from Rahway, put it: "When you view the program and review the statistics that have been collected, there is no doubt in my mind . . . that the juvenile awareness project at Rahway State prison is perhaps today the most effective, inexpensive deterrent in the entire correctional process in America."[5]

But there turned out to be one rather large problem with Scared Straight. It didn't work. Rigorous testing would later prove that the kids who were taken on prison visits were *more likely* to commit offenses in the future, not less—as we shall see. A more appropriate name for Scared Straight might have been Scared Crooked. It was an unequivocal failure. It damaged kids in a number of ways.

But first we will ask: How is this possible? How can something be a failure when the statistics seem to show that it is a success? How can it be failing when virtually every expert is lining up to endorse it? To answer that question we will examine one of the most important scientific innovations of the last two hundred years, and one that takes us to the heart of the closed-loop phenomenon—and how to overcome it.

The randomized control trial.

II

C losed loops are often perpetuated by people covering up mistakes. They are also kept in place when people spin their mistakes, rather than confronting them head on. But there is a third way that closed loops are sustained over time: through skewed interpretation.

That was the problem that bedeviled bloodletting, practiced by medieval doctors. The doctors had what seemed like clear feedback on what worked and what didn't. Either the patient died in the aftermath of the procedure or did not. The evidence was there for all to see.

But how to interpret this evidence? As we've seen, doctors, already convinced of the wisdom of figures like Galen, trusted in the power of bloodletting. When a patient died, it was because they were so ill that not even bloodletting could save them. But when they lived, that confirmed the brilliance of the procedure.

Think of how many success stories must have been circulating around the medieval world: people who had been terribly ill, close to death perhaps, but bloodletting had been performed, and they had recovered. How persuasive their testimony would have sounded. "I was on the brink of mortality, a doctor drained me of some blood, and now I am cured!"

Consider how they would have commended the procedure in market squares. Those who died on the other hand? Well, they would not be around to say anything, would they? Their testimony had vanished.

Now look at the following diagram.[6]

In this (hypothetical) example, a group of chronically ill people are subjected to bloodletting. Some of them recover. This is the "evidence" that justifies the treatment. People get better and they are understandably happy about it.

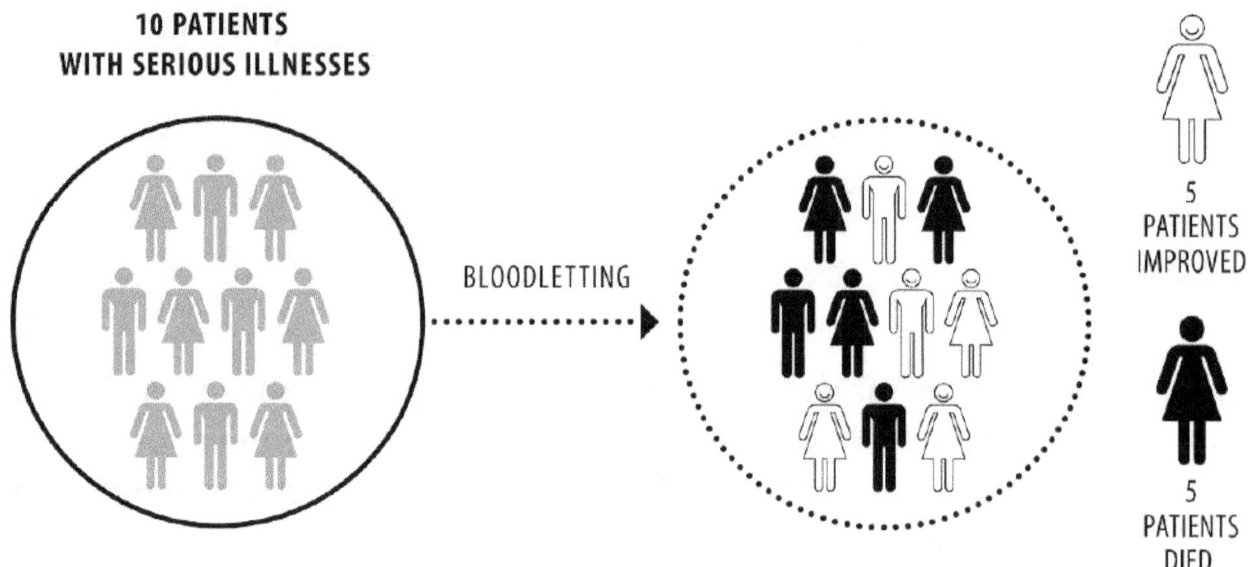

Bloodletting without a control group.

However, what the doctors don't see, and the patients don't see, is what would have happened if the treatment had *not been given*. In experiments this is commonly known as the "counterfactual." It is all the things that *could* have happened but which in everyday experience we never observe because we did something else.

We don't observe what would have happened if we had not gotten married. Or see what would have happened if we had taken a different job. We can speculate on what would have happened, and we can make decent guesses. But we don't really know. This may seem like a trivial point, but the implications are profound.

Now look at another diagram, below. Here the patients have been randomly divided into two groups. Some of them get access to bloodletting while the others (called the control group) do not. This is known as a randomized control trial (RTC); in medicine it is called a clinical trial. We see from the diagram that many of the patients who receive bloodletting recover. It looks successful. The feedback is impressive.

But now look at the group who did not get the treatment. Many more have recovered than in the treated group. The reason is simple: the body has its own powers of recuperation. People recover naturally even without treatment. In fact, by comparing the two groups, it is possible to see that, far from saving people as medieval doctors sincerely believed, bloodletting, on average, kills them. This fact would have been invisible without the control group.* And this is why, as we noted in chapter 1, bloodletting survived as a recognized treatment until the nineteenth century.

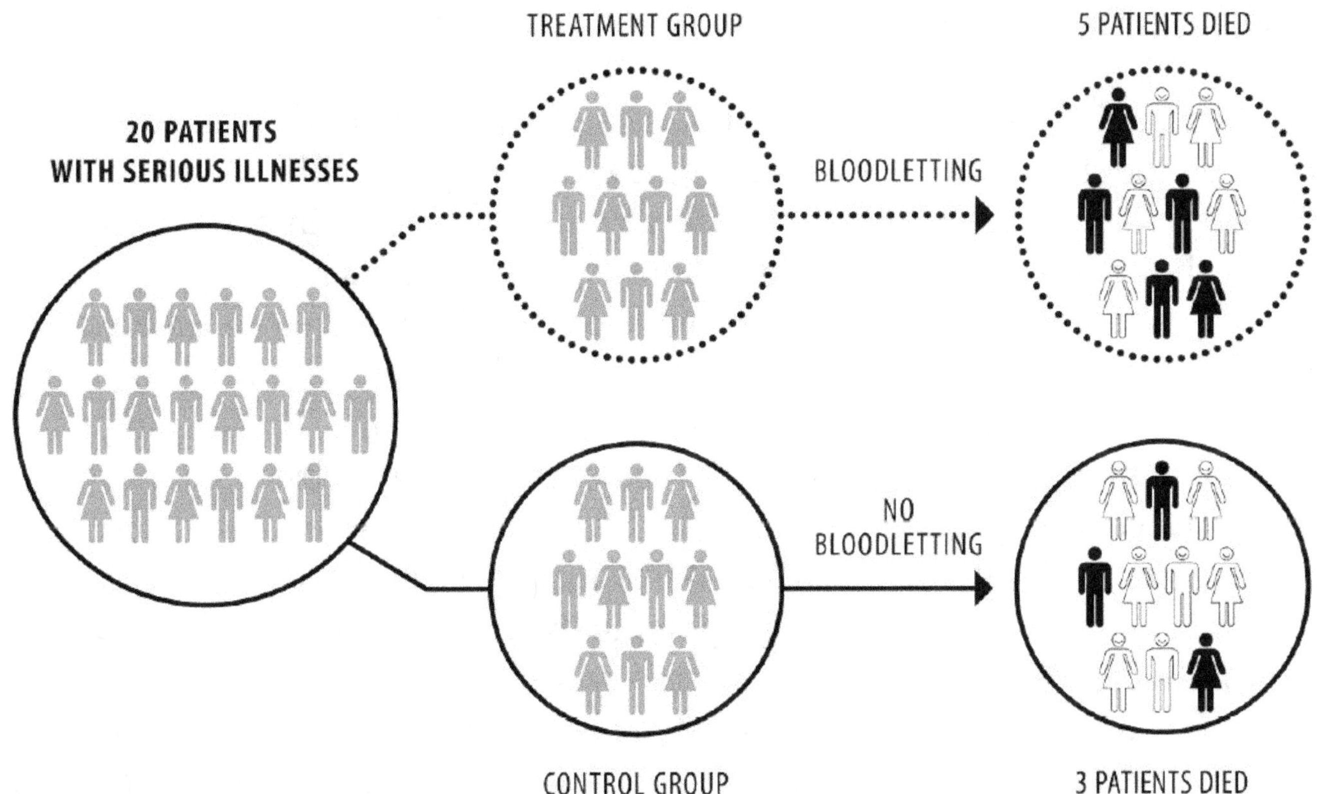

Bloodletting with a control group.

So far in this book we have examined cases of unambiguous error. When a plane crashes you know the procedures were defective. When DNA evidence shows that an innocent man is convicted, you know the trial or investigation was flawed. When a minimum viable product is rejected by early adopters, you can be sure the final product will bomb. When a nozzle is clogging up, you know it will cost you money. These examples gave us a chance to examine failure in the raw.

Much real-world failure is not like this. Often, failure is clouded in ambiguity. What looks like success may really be failure and vice versa. And this, in turn, represents a serious obstacle to progress. After all, how can you learn from failure if you are not sure you have actually failed? Or, to put it in the language of the last chapter, how can you drive evolution without a clear selection mechanism?

To take a concrete example, suppose you redesign your company website and that sales subsequently increase. That might lead you to believe that the redesign of the website caused the boost in sales. After all, one preceded the other. But how can you be sure? Perhaps sales went up not because of the new website, but because a rival went bust, or interest rates went down, or because it was a rainy month and more people shopped online. Indeed, it is entirely possible that sales would have gone up even more if you had *not* changed the website.

Looking at the sales statistics is not going to help you find an answer any more than looking at the number of people recovering from bloodletting will help you find out if the treatment is effective. The reason is simple: you can't observe the counterfactual. You don't know whether the change in sales was caused by something else; something, perhaps, you hadn't even considered.

RCTs solve this problem. In effect they provide a high-definition test. They turn shades of gray into something closer to black and white. By isolating the relationship between an intervention (bloodletting, a new website, etc.) and an outcome (recovery from illness, sales) without it being obscured by other influences, they clarify the feedback. Without such a test you could draw the wrong conclusions, not just once but potentially indefinitely.

RCTs have revolutionized pharmacology. Ben Goldacre, a doctor and writer who is an evangelist for evidence-based medicine, has said: "This one idea has probably saved more lives, on a more spectacular scale, than any other idea you will come across this year."[7] Mark Henderson, a former science editor of *The Times*, said: "The Randomised Control Trial is one of the greatest inventions of modern science."[8]

It is probably worth emphasizing that RCTs are not a panacea. There are situations where they are difficult to use and where they might be considered unethical. And trials have often been rigged in subtle ways by pharmaceutical companies eager to come up with an answer that they have already prejudged.[9] But these are not arguments against randomized trials, merely against how they have been corrupted by people with dubious motives.

Another objection is that randomized trials neglect the holistic nature of a system. In medicine, for example, while a drug may cure a particular symptom, it may also have negative long-term effects on the rest of the body, or leave the underlying cause untreated. For example, prescribing a pill to combat a stomach complaint might cause damage to the immune system that could, in the long run, leave the patient worse off.

What this objection is saying, in effect, is that the measurement period for a clinical trial shouldn't be the immediate aftermath of administering a drug, but the entire life of the patient, and that the outcome shouldn't merely focus on a particular symptom, but the whole person. This shows that it is vital to keep an eye on the long-term consequences when conducting RCTs, something that has sometimes been overlooked in medicine.

But it is also worth noting that such considerations carry little weight when it comes to life-threatening conditions. If you find yourself in the middle of an epidemic of, for example, smallpox or Ebola, you will want the vaccine even if there is a risk of complications in a few decades' time.[10]

With these caveats in mind, then, RCTs offer a powerful method of establishing rigorous tests in a complex world. Handled with care, they cut through the ambiguity that can play havoc with our interpretation of feedback. And they are often simple to conduct.

Take the example of the redesigned website mentioned earlier. The problem was in establishing whether the change in the design had increased sales, or was caused by something else. But suppose you randomly direct users to either the new or the old design. You could then measure whether they buy more goods from the former or the latter. This would filter out all the other influences such as interest rates, competition, weather and so on, and reveal the hidden counterfactual.

There have been around half a million RCTs in medicine since the 1950s. They have saved hundreds of thousands of lives. But the remarkable thing is that in many areas of human life RCTs have hardly been used at all. In the criminal justice system they are almost nonexistent. In 2006, for example, there were almost 25,000 trials in medicine, but in crime and justice across the world there were only 85 between 1982 and 2004.[11]

David Halpern, one of the most respected policy analysts in the UK, has said: "Many areas of government have not been tested in any form whatsoever. They are based on hunch, gut feel and narrative. The same is true of many areas outside government. We are effectively flying blind, without much of a clue as to what really works, and what doesn't. It is actually quite scary."[12]

Closed loops are not merely an intellectual curiosity, they realistically describe the world we live in. They are small and large, subtle and intricate; they lurk in small companies, big companies, charities, corporations and governments. The majority of our assumptions have never been subject to robust failure tests. Unless we do something about it they never will be.

To glimpse the often mind-bending gulf between what we think we know and what we really know, let us revisit the Scared Straight program. It looked astonishingly effective. The observational statistics seemed compelling.* But we now know that the program was increasing crime rather than reducing it.

In many ways, Scared Straight stands as a metaphor not merely for government policy (perhaps the closest thing in the twentieth-first century to bloodletting), but for the wider world. This program could have continued on its merry way for decades, perhaps centuries, without a proper test.

Scared Straight is a metaphor, but above all, it is a warning.

III

In 1999, *Scared Straight! 20 Years Later* was broadcast in the United States. The documentary was fronted this time by Danny Glover rather than Peter Falk, and revisited those seventeen, scrawny teenagers who had appeared in the original film. The results were as seemingly miraculous as the original program had led audiences to believe.

Many of the interviewees talked about their new lives. Almost all credited the three-hour visit to Rahway two decades earlier as having turned their lives around. Terence, the young black kid who had once stolen cars and broken into stores, was now a part-time preacher at his local Baptist church, with a wife and two sons. "Chances are, if I wouldn't have gone to Rahway, I would probably be locked up and could be in my grave," he said.

Lori, the sixteen-year-old with the wide smile and big earrings, who had been dealing drugs, was now a thirty-six-year-old bookkeeper and mother. "I just thought it was a day away from school," she said. "I don't think I have ever been as afraid in my whole life . . . It made me not want to be an idiot anymore . . . I started going to school more after that."

Angelo, the kid with the unkempt hair and wispy mustache, was now thirty-seven years old, tiled floors for a living and had three kids. He said "If I didn't go to Rahway, I think I would have done hard time," he said. "If that one day didn't happen, I might not have my family. And my family to me right now is everything; it is the most beautiful experience in the world."

This, then, is how the phenomenon of Scared Straight looked to millions of TV viewers. The statistics look good, too. This was a scheme, unlike most social programs, that actually bothered to collect data. According to the evidence, around 80 to 90 percent of people who attended the program went straight. As stated in the documentary: "That is an amazing success story. And it is unequalled by traditional rehabilitation methods."

But if we rewind to the late spring of 1977, a rather different picture was starting to emerge. In April of that year, James Finckenauer, a professor at the Rutgers School of Criminal Justice, decided to test Scared Straight. He wasn't just interested in the observational statistics. As a scientist he knew that these could be misleading. He was not interested in hype or slickly presented documentaries either. He wanted to know if the scheme *really* worked. In short, he wanted to run an RCT.

Finckenauer has silver-white hair and inquiring eyes. He has published dozens of papers and won multiple awards for his research, but his most striking quality is his conversational style. He is cautious, considered, and attentive. He also has a laserlike quality, as if he is trying to cut through the surface to find the truths lying beneath. These qualities would serve him well as he forensically unpicked the Scared Straight phenomenon.

Before starting the RCT, Finckenauer probed the existing evidence for Scared Straight. Where did the 80 to 90 percent figure for kids going straight come from? He found that it was based on a questionnaire sent to the parents or guardians of children who had visited Rahway. (Another source of the data was letters of commendation sent in by the sponsoring agencies which brought kids to Rahway. These were not terribly reliable. These agencies may have had all sorts of hidden incentives to believe in the program.)

There were four yes-or-no questions:

> Have you noticed a marked change in your child's conduct since their visit to the prison?
>
> Has there been a slight change in their behavior since their visit to prison?
>
> Do you think another visit is necessary for your son/daughter?
>
> Are there any specific areas you think we might be of some assistance to you, or your son or daughter?

There was also space to write comments.[13]

But what did a "marked" change actually mean? What did a "slight" change mean? The questions were open to all kinds of interpretation. Finckenauer also discovered that many of the kids who visited Rahway had not been delinquent or even pre-delinquent in the first place. It hardly counts as a success that they didn't commit crime afterward if they were already on the straight and narrow. Furthermore, the letters to parents were often sent within weeks of the prison visit. That was scarcely enough time to judge a change in behavior.

And yet these were only minor quibbles. The deeper flaws go to the heart of what constitutes valid evidence. The first is that only those who responded to the questionnaire were included in the statistics. Those who didn't respond were entirely absent from the data. Consider how that might have distorted the result. It is possible that only the parents of children whose behavior improved bothered to respond. Parents whose kids continued to behave badly might have thrown the questionnaire in the bin, or at least responded in fewer numbers. This could have skewed the stats beyond recognition.

This is a type of so-called "selection bias" and it should sound familiar. It is pretty much the same problem that bedeviled medieval medicine when only those who recovered from bloodletting were able to testify to its effectiveness. The evidence sounded terrific but that is because it was dangerously incomplete. Those who did not recover from bloodletting were never given a chance to express an opinion. Why? Because they were already dead.

The deepest problem with the Scared Straight statistics, however, related to the counterfactual. Even if everyone *had* responded to the questionnaire (which they hadn't), we still wouldn't know whether the outcomes had been caused by the intervention or by something else. Perhaps behavior would have improved without the intervention. Perhaps it improved because the local economy was improving, or because of a new scheme at school, or some other factor. Perhaps the outcome would have been even better *without* the intervention.

In August 1978, Finckenauer divided a set of delinquent youths into two random groups.[*] One group attended the Scared Straight program. The other group (the control group) did not. He then sat and waited to measure the results. Despite the hype, the stellar-looking stats, the slick PR, the Oscar-winning documentary, the commendations from politicians, the tributes from corrections officers, and the widespread adoption of the scheme around the world, this was the first time the project had been subjected to the most rigorous kind of failure test.

And the results, when they finally arrived, were dramatic. Scared Straight didn't work. The children who attended Rahway were more likely to commit crimes than those who did not. "The evidence showed that the kids who went on the program were at greater risk of offending than those who didn't," Finckenauer said. "The data when you compared the treatment and control group was clear."

This was, to many people, a surprise. The program looked good. The logic seemed compelling. It had parents lining up to say that it had "cured" their kids.

The questionnaire data seemed solid, too. But all of these things were true of bloodletting. Only with an RCT could we cut through the ambiguity and see the real effect of the program.

Finckenauer says:

> People were convinced of the success of Scared Straight because it seemed so intuitive. People loved the idea that kids could be turned around through a tough session with a group of lifers. But crime turns out to be more complex than that. Children commit offenses for many different, often subtle reasons. With hindsight, a three-hour visit to prison was unlikely to solve the problem.
>
> The intentions of the inmates were genuine: they really wanted the kids to go straight. But the program was having unintended consequences. The experience of being shouted at seemed to be brutalizing the youngsters. Many seemed to be going out and committing crime just to prove to themselves and their peers that they weren't really scared.[14]

Defenders of the scheme reacted angrily to Finckenauer's report. Judge Nicola, who had lavishly praised the program in the documentary, said: ". . . the [Scared Straight] program doesn't need defending." Robert J. McAlesher, the staff adviser to Scared Straight, was even more blistering. "We question the motives of dilettantes [i.e., Finckenauer] who compromise their intellectual integrity by thrusting themselves into the national limelight with meaningless statistics deceptively presented as the result of scientific study."[15]

These responses were, in a sense, predictable. When we are presented with evidence that challenges our deeply held beliefs, we tend to reject the evidence or shoot the messenger rather than amend our beliefs. Indeed, many of the defenders of Scared Straight responded to the results of Finckenauer's RCT by saying that they had become *more convinced* of the efficacy of the program, not less. This is precisely what the theory of cognitive dissonance would predict.

But even those with no prior commitment to Scared Straight continued to be attracted to the program, like moths to a flame. The hard data showed that it was counterproductive, but the narrative of kids being deterred from crime by mean-talking inmates was too seductive to ignore. By the 1980s, Scared Straight–style programs were in operation in Georgia, South Carolina, and Wisconsin. Further programs were set up in New York, Virginia, Alaska, Ohio, and Michigan.[16]

It was as if the research conducted by Finckenauer had never happened.

By the 1990s similar programs were burgeoning. The Los Angeles Police Department ran a scheme where one of the components was kids visiting the city prison to be "shouted and screamed at" by convicts. At a program in Carson City, Nevada, a youngster was reported as saying that the part of the tour that made the greatest impact was "all the inmates calling us for sex and fighting for our belongings." The idea was soon exported to the UK, Australia, and Norway.

Meanwhile, the hard evidence against the scheme was multiplying. RCTs were conducted on Scared Straight–style programs from the West to the East Coast of America. They found the same thing: Scared Straight doesn't work. It often damages kids. One of the trials showed a 25 percent increase in delinquency in the treatment group compared with the control group.

But none of this seemed to matter. The glitzy narrative was far more seductive than the boring old data.[17]

Even government officials eulogized the program. In 1994, a Scared Straight–style scheme in Ohio was commended in the official publication of the U.S. Office of Juvenile Justice and Delinquency Prevention. The experts had been bewitched by the narrative fallacy. In 1996, almost twenty years after Finckenauer's RCT, the *New York Times* reported that the original program at Rahway was at the height of its popularity, hosting around ten groups per week or 12,500 kids per year.

But then in 2002 the Campbell Collaboration arrived on the scene. This is a global, nonprofit organization devoted to evidence-based policy. They conducted what is called a "systematic review." This is where the data from all the randomized trials are collated into a single spreadsheet. By pooling the results from all the individual trials (seven were used in the so-called meta-analysis), a systematic review represents the gold standard when it comes to scientific evidence. It is the ultimate failure test.[18]

Forgive me if you know what's coming, but the results were emphatic. Scared Straight doesn't work. It increases crime. Some research indicates that this increase can be as high as 28 percent.[19] In exquisitely understated language, the authors effectively damned its entire rationale: "We conclude that programs like Scared Straight are likely to have a harmful effect and increase delinquency . . . Doing nothing would have been better than exposing juveniles to the program."[20]

Scared Straight was, in many ways, ahead of its time. Unlike most social programs, which collate no data whatsoever, it actually sent out questionnaires and gathered statistics. But, as with medieval bloodletting, observational stats do not always provide reliable data. Often, you need to test the counterfactual. Otherwise you may be harming people without even realizing it.

And this is really the point. It doesn't require people to be actively deceitful or negligent for mistakes to be perpetuated. Sometimes it can happen in plain view of the evidence, because people either don't know how to, or are subconsciously unwilling to, interrogate the data.

But how often do we actually test our policies and strategies? How often do we probe our assumptions, in life or at work? In medicine, as we have seen, there have been almost one million randomized trials. In criminal justice, they scarcely exist. Policy, almost across the board, is run on narrative, hunch, untested ideology, and observational data skewed to fit predetermined conclusions.

Closed loops are not just an intellectual curiosity, they accurately (and sometimes terrifyingly) describe the world in which we live.

• • •

On January 1, 1982, an intruder broke into the home of a nineteen-year-old called Michele Mika. After rummaging through several rooms, he took a knife from the kitchen, entered Ms. Mika's bedroom, and murdered her. Michele's mother later found her facedown in bed with an eight-inch carving knife in her back. After she was killed, Ms. Mika was sexually assaulted for several hours. The motive was pure sexual gratification.[21]

More than twenty-five years later, on March 17, 2007, police arrested Angelo Speziale, a forty-five-year-old living in Hackensack, New Jersey. Speziale was one of the original seventeen youngsters profiled in *Scared Straight!* He was the kid with the unkempt hair and wispy mustache who had robbed shops in the neighborhood. He had also been interviewed in the follow-up feature twenty years later, by which time he had three kids and a job tiling floors.

Like most of the people interviewed for the follow-up program, Speziale claimed that the visit to Rahway had transformed his life. It sounded almost inspirational. "If I didn't go to Rahway, I think I would have done hard time," he said. Danny Glover, the narrator, said: "Angelo, thirty-seven, is now a law-abiding family man."

But the reality was rather different. In 2005, Speziale was arrested for shoplifting and police obtained a DNA sample. During routine testing they discovered that it matched the DNA of the sperm found in the corpse of Michele Mika. Mika and Speziale, it turned out, had lived on opposite sides of the same duplex on Teaneck Avenue at the time the murder had taken place.

The makers of the documentary did not deliberately mislead audiences about Speziale. They couldn't have known that he was deceiving them when he said he had "gone straight." They couldn't have realized that just three years after he had visited Rahway, he had raped and murdered an innocent nineteen-year-old. Only the test provided by DNA revealed the truth.

But the documentary makers did know by the early 1980s that Scared Straight was increasing crime. And yet they continued to make celebratory programs on the project. A&E, an American cable and satellite channel, introduced *Beyond Scared Straight*, a new series, in 2011. By 2014 it was in its eighth season. Arnold Shapiro, the producer (who also made the original 1978 documentary), continues to defend the scheme, despite the overwhelming evidence against it. He argues that Scared Straight today involves more counseling and less shouting. But the logic of conducting the interventions in prisons has always relied on a confrontational component. As the *Daily Beast* put it:

> The episodes themselves do emphasize the horrors of prison life more than discussion. At the beginning of one filmed at Maryland's Jessup prison, a 50-year-old man convicted of first-degree murder barks into a 17-year-old dropout's face, "Don't smile at another man in prison, 'cause if you smile at another man in prison, that makes them think that you like them, and for you to like another man in prison, something seriously is wrong with you."

In his three-hour visit to Rahway in 1978, Speziale endured a number of degradations, but one event is particularly chilling in hindsight. The youngster was forced to stand in front of the group and read out a newspaper report of a knife attack that had taken place in prison. "Rahway inmate stabbed to death in cell block," the sixteen-year-old read, voice trembling. "He was stabbed about a dozen times in the neck, chest, head and back. Robinson was pronounced dead on arrival at Rahway General Hospital."

There is no evidence of any connection between the fact that Speziale was humiliated into reading out loud the details of a savage knife attack on his visit to Rahway in 1978 and the fact that he perpetrated a similar crime a few years later. This is almost certainly a coincidence. But what we do know is that these visits, on average, damage the kids who are taken on them. We have known that for more than three decades.

In 2010, Speziale pleaded guilty to sexual assault and stabbing and was sentenced to twenty-five years.[22] He is now back in Rahway prison, where this story began. It is an endlessly disturbing and cautionary tale. But the deepest irony of all, and the one that takes us to the heart of the closed-loop phenomenon, is that Speziale might soon be delivering Scared Straight–style confrontations to the next generation of delinquents.[*]

Part IV
SMALL STEPS AND GIANT LEAPS

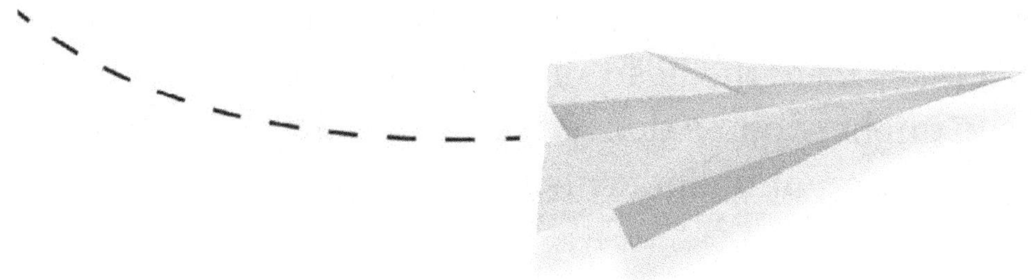

Chapter 9

Marginal Gains

I

A t around 9 a.m. the riders of Team Sky, the British professional cycling team, made their way out of a small hotel in Carcassonne, a beautiful town in the Languedoc-Roussillon region of southern France. It was a warm morning and the riders walked to the team bus in silence, contemplating the day to come.

They were about to start Stage 16 of the 2014 Tour de France, one of the sternest tests of endurance in the sporting world. They had already ridden 3,000 kilometers over the preceding fifteen stages and now faced a 237.5-kilometer ride culminating at the feared Port de Balès, a 19-kilometer climb into the Pyrenees. "Here we go again," Bernhard Eisel, one of the team members, said with a grim smile.

On the Team Sky bus there was a sense of anticipation. The riders were getting into their sports gear. The coaches were reviewing race plans. With thirty minutes to go, Nicolas Portal, one of Team Sky's sporting directors, began his pre-race briefing. He talked about the importance of the stage and alerted the riders to difficult sections along the route. As he did so photographs of tough corners and steep climbs were flashed onto a screen at the front of the bus.

As he finished his talk, a man toward the back, silent until that moment, started to speak. He had a shaved head, dark-rimmed glasses and an intense manner. He is the man who always has the final word before the race: the general manager of Team Sky, Sir David Brailsford.

"At the end of the day, success is about getting in the breakaway [where a group of cyclists ride away from the main pack]," he said. "Let's not f*** about. Either we are in it or we are not. I know it is difficult. I know how hard it is. But everyone needs to buy into this. All focus on that. That is our goal for today. The rest will look after itself. Don't let anyone else make it happen; make it happen for yourselves . . . OK, hit it!"

A quiet buzz reverberated around the bus. Brailsford had struck the right note. All eight riders stood up and exchanged glances. They then made their way down the steps to the starting line of the sixteenth stage.

. . .

The previous evening Brailsford had given me a tour of the Team Sky operation. We looked at the trucks, the design of the team bus, and the detailed algorithms that are used to track the performance of each cyclist. It was an opportunity to glimpse behind the curtains of one of the most admired and tightly policed operations in all sport.

The success of Brailsford is legendary. When he joined British track cycling as an adviser in 1997, the team was behind the curve. In 2000 Great Britain won a single Olympic gold medal in the time trial. In 2004, one year after Brailsford was appointed performance director, Britain won two Olympic gold medals. In 2008 they won an astonishing eight gold medals and, at the London Olympics in 2012, repeated the feat.

Meanwhile, something even more remarkable was happening. Track cycling is competitive, but the most prestigious form of the sport is professional road cycling. Britain had never had a winner of the Tour de France since the race was established in 1903. British riders had won individual stages, but nobody had come close to winning the general classification.

But in 2009, even as the British track cycling team was preparing for the London Olympics, Brailsford embarked upon a new challenge. He created a road cycling team, Team Sky, while continuing to oversee the track team. On the day the new outfit was announced to the world, Brailsford also announced that they would win the Tour de France within five years.

Most people laughed at this aspiration. One commentator said: "Brailsford has set himself up for an almighty fall." But in 2012, two years ahead of schedule, Bradley Wiggins became the first-ever British rider to win the event. The following year, Team Sky triumphed again when Chris Froome, another Brit, won the general classification. It was widely acclaimed as one of the most extraordinary feats in British sporting history.

How did it happen? How did Brailsford conquer not one cycling discipline, but two? These were the questions I asked him over dinner at the team's small hotel after the tour of the facilities.

His answer was clear: "It is about marginal gains," he said. "The approach comes from the idea that if you break down a big goal into small parts, and then improve on each of them, you will deliver a huge increase when you put them all together."

It sounds simple, but as a philosophy, marginal gains has become one of the hottest concepts not just in sports, but beyond. It has formed the basis of business conferences, and seminars and has even been debated in the armed forces. Many British sports now employ a director of marginal gains.

But what does this philosophy actually mean in practice? How do you deliver a marginal gains approach, not just in sport, but in other organizations? Most significantly of all, why does breaking a big project into smaller parts help you to tackle really ambitious goals?

To glimpse an answer, let us leave cycling for a moment and look at a very different area of life. For it turns out that the best way to grasp the meaning of marginal gains is to examine one of the most pressing issues facing the world today: global poverty.

II

Take a look at the graph here.[1] It is reproduced from the work of Esther Duflo, one of the world's most respected economists, currently working out of MIT.

The vertical, light-gray bars show the amount of aid spending on Africa over the last thirty years. As you can see, the funding has gradually increased since the early 1960s, peaking at almost $800 million in 2006. The investment has a simple imperative: to improve the lives of the world's poorest. It is an important objective given that 25,000 children die of preventable causes every day.[2]

The key question here is, Did the investment make a difference? Did it improve the lives of the people it was designed to help?

A sensible place to start when answering that question is with African GDP. In the diagram African GDP is shown by the solid black line. As you can see, this has stayed roughly constant over the period. This might lead one to the conclusion that all the aid spending hasn't done much good. It hasn't boosted economic activity. It hasn't raised the living standards of those living in Africa. In fact it all seems like an expensive waste of time.

But the insights from the previous chapter should urge a little caution. Why? Because the data don't give us an insight into the counterfactual. Perhaps the aid spending was incredibly successful. Perhaps, without it, GDP in Africa would have been far lower—the white line in the graph.

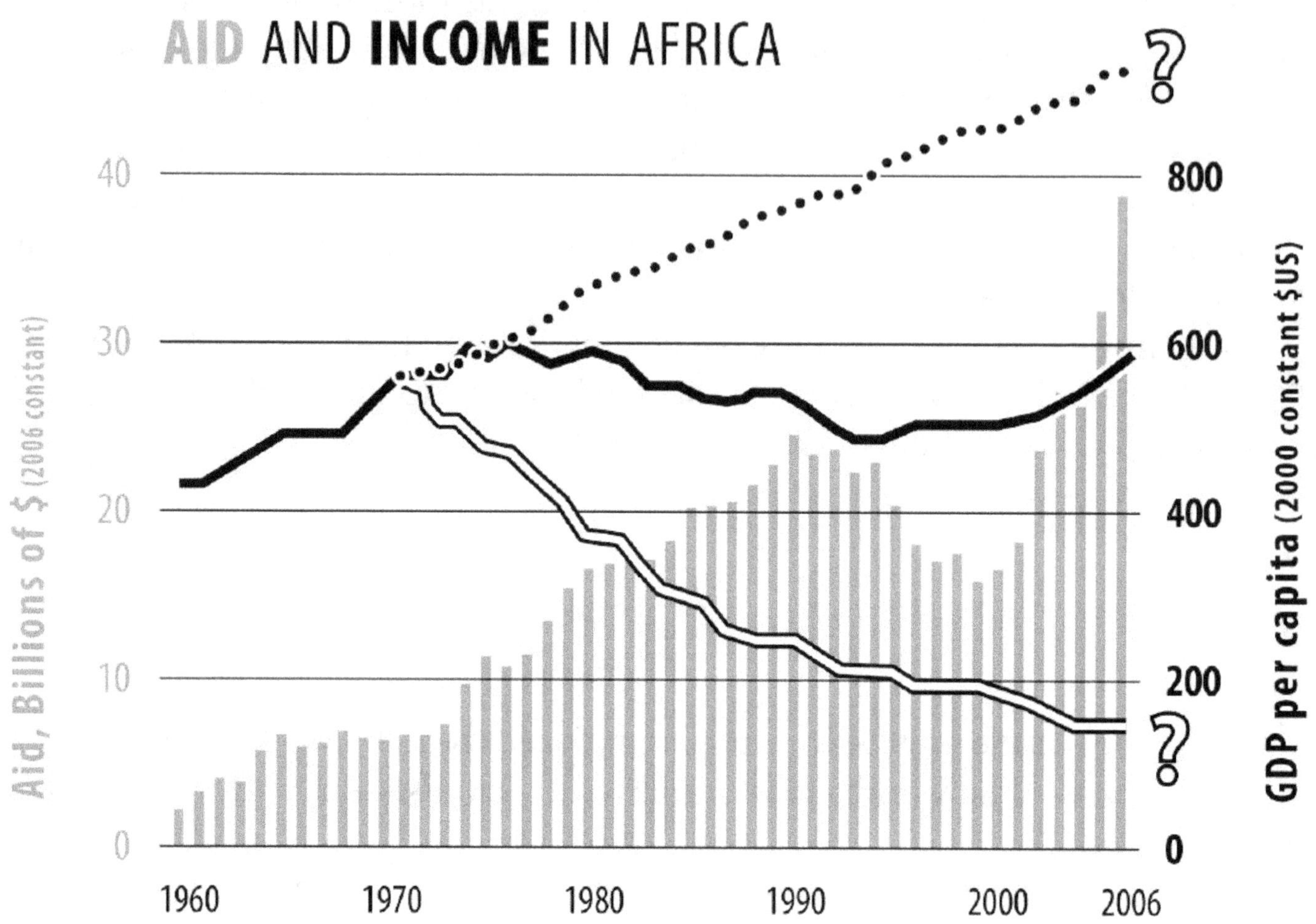

Of course, there is another possibility. Perhaps aid spending was even more detrimental than the solid black line might lead you to believe. Perhaps it was a disaster, destroying incentives, boosting corruption, and lowering growth below what it would otherwise have been. Perhaps without it Africa would have actually surged ahead: as per the dotted line in the graph. How can we know either way?

Each of these two alternatives has high-profile supporters. Jeffrey Sachs, director of the Earth Institute at Columbia University, for example, is a vocal advocate of development spending. He argues that aid has benefited the lives of Africans and claims that more money could eradicate poverty altogether. *The End of Poverty*, his best-selling book, is based in part upon this premise.[3]

Conversely, William Easterly, an economist at New York University, profoundly disagrees. He argues that aid spending has had all sorts of negative side effects, and that Africa would have been better off without it. His book *The White Man's Burden* presents this case with as much intellectual force as that of Sachs.[4]

The best way to adjudicate between these stances would be to conduct a randomized control trial. This would enable us to isolate the effect of development spending from all the other influences on African GDP. But there is a rather obvious problem. There is only one Africa. You cannot find lots of different Africas, randomly divide them into groups, give aid to some and not to others, and then measure the outcomes.

This may sound like a trivial point, but it has wider implications. When it comes to really big issues, it is very difficult to conduct controlled experiments. To run an RCT you need a control group, which is not easy when the unit of analysis is very large. This applies to many things beyond development aid, such as climate change (there is only one world), issues of war and peace, and the like.

This brings us directly to the concept of marginal gains. If the answer to a big question is difficult to establish, why not break it down into lots of smaller questions? After all, aid spending has many subcomponents. There are programs on malaria, literacy, road-building, education, and infrastructure, each of them constructed in different ways, with different kinds of incentives, and delivered by different organizations.

At this level of magnification, by looking at one program at a time, it is perfectly possible to run controlled experiments. You try out the program with some people or communities, but not with others, and then compare the two groups to see if it is working or not. Instead of debating whether aid is working *as a whole* (a debate that is very difficult to settle on the basis of observational data), you can find definitive answers at the smaller level and build back up from there.

To examine a concrete example, suppose you were trying to improve educational outcomes in Africa. One way to see if aid spending is working would be to look at the correlation between the quantity of spending and the average grade score across the continent. The problem is that this wouldn't give you any information about the counterfactual (what would have happened to scores without the funding).

But now suppose that instead of looking at the big picture, you examine an individual program. That is precisely what a group of pioneering economists did in the impoverished Busia and Teso regions in the west of Kenya. As the author Tim Harford points out in his book *Adapt,* these economists wanted to know whether handing out free textbooks to schools would boost grades. Intuitively, they were pretty sure it would. In the past the observational data had been good. Schools that received books tended to improve their test scores.

But the economists wanted to be sure, so they performed an RCT. Instead of giving the textbooks to the most deserving schools, which is the common approach, they randomly divided a number of eligible schools into two groups: one group received free textbooks and the other group did not. Now, the charity had a treatment group and a control group. They had a chance to examine whether the books were making a real difference.

The results, when they came in, were both emphatic and surprising. The students in the schools that received free textbooks didn't perform any better than those who did not. The test results in the two groups of schools were almost identical. This outcome contradicted intuition and the observational data. But then randomized trials often do.

The problem, it turned out, was not the books, but the language they were written in. English is the third language of most of the poor children living in remote Busia and Teso. They were struggling to grasp the material as it was presented. Researchers might not have realized this had they not run a trial. It pierced through to one of the untested assumptions in their approach.

Confronted with failure, the economists tried another approach. They conducted another randomized trial but instead of using textbooks they used visual aids. These were flipcharts with bold graphics that covered geography, math, *etc.* Again, the economists expected them to boost test scores. And again, when they compared the test scores in the treatment group with those of the control group, the flipcharts were a failure. They led to no significant improvement in learning.

Undeterred, the economists started to think about the problem in a fresh way. They tried something completely new: a de-worming medication. This may seem like a curious way to improve education, but researchers were aware that these parasites stunt growth, cause children to feel lethargic, and lead to absenteeism. They disproportionately affect children in remote communities, just like those in Busia and Teso.

This time the results were excellent. They vastly exceeded the expectations of the researchers. As Tim Harford put it: "The program was a huge success, boosting children's height, reducing re-infection rates, and also reducing absenteeism from school by a quarter. And it was cheap."[5]

This was a marginal gain. It was just one program in one small region. But by looking at education at this level of magnification, it was possible to see what really works, and what doesn't. The economists had tested, failed, and learned. They could now roll it out in other areas, while continuing to test, and iterate, and create yet more marginal gains.

This may sound like a gradual way to improve, but look at the alternative. Consider what would have happened if the economists had relied on intuition and observational data. They might have continued with free textbooks forever, deluding themselves that they were making a difference, when they were doing virtually nothing at all.

This approach is now the focus of a crusading group of economists who have transformed international development over the last decade. They do not come up with grand designs; rather, they look for small advantages. As Esther Duflo, the French-born economist who is at the forefront of this approach, put it: "If we don't know if we are doing any good, we are not any better than the medieval doctors and their leeches. Sometimes the patient gets better; sometimes the patient dies. Is it the leeches or something else? We don't know."[6]

Critics of randomized trials often worry about the morality of "experimenting on people." Why should one group get X while another is getting Y? Shouldn't everyone have access to the best possible treatment? Put like this, RCTs may seem unethical. But now think about it in a different way. If you are genuinely unsure which policy is the most effective, it is only by running a trial that you can find out. The alternative is not morally neutral, it simply means that you never learn. In the long run this helps nobody.

Duflo, who is petite and dynamic, doesn't regard her work as lacking in ambition; rather, she regards these incremental improvements as pioneering. She told me:

It is very easy to sit back and come up with grand theories about how to change the world. But often our intuitions are wrong. The world is too complex to figure everything out from your armchair. The only way to be sure is to go out and test your ideas and programs, and to realize that you will often be wrong. But that is not a bad thing. It leads to progress.

This links back to the work of Toby Ord, whom we met in chapter 7. He uses the data discovered by the likes of Duflo to advise private individuals on where to donate their money. He realized that relying on hunch and narrative can mean that millions of pounds are squandered on ineffective programs. And this is why hundreds of controlled experiments are now being conducted across the developing world. Each test demonstrates whether a policy or program works, or if it doesn't.

Each test provides a small gain of one kind or another (remember that failure is not inherently bad: it sets the stage for new ideas). By breaking a big problem into smaller parts, it is easier to cut through narrative fallacies. You fail more, but you learn more.

As Duflo puts it: "It is possible to make significant progress against the biggest problem in the world through the accumulation of a set of small steps, each well thought out, carefully tested, and judiciously implemented."[7]

III

And this takes us back to David Brailsford and British cycling. Note the similarity of the final quote of Duflo with that of Brailsford earlier in this chapter. "The whole approach comes from the idea that if you break down a big goal into small parts, and then improve on each of them, you will gain a huge increase when you put them all together."

Cycling is very different from international development, but the success of its most pioneering coach is based on the same conceptual insight. As Brailsford puts it: "I realized early on that having a grand strategy was futile on its own. You also have to look at a smaller level, figure out what is working and what isn't. Each step may be small, but the aggregation can be huge."

Running controlled trials in cycling is significantly easier than in development aid, not least because the aim of the sport is relatively simple: getting from A to B as quickly as possible. To obtain the most efficient bicycle design, for example, British cycling created a wind tunnel. This enabled them to isolate the aerodynamic effect, by varying the design of the bike and testing it in identical conditions. To discover the most efficient training methods, Brailsford created new data sets that enabled him to track every subcomponent of physiological performance.

"Each gain on its own was small," Brailsford said. "But that doesn't really matter. We were getting a deeper understanding of each aspect of performance. It was the difference between trailing behind the rest of the world and coming first."

In *Corporate Creativity*, the authors Alan Robinson and Sam Stern write of how Bob Crandall, the former chairman of American Airlines, removed a single olive from every salad, and in doing so saved $500,000 annually.[8] Many seized on this as a marginal gain. But was it? After all, if removing an olive is a good idea, why not the lettuce too? At what point does an exercise in incremental cost-cutting start to impact on the bottom line?

Now we can see a clear answer. Marginal gains is not about making small changes and hoping they fly. Rather, it is about breaking down a big problem into small parts in order to rigorously establish what works and what doesn't. Ultimately the approach emerges from a basic property of empirical evidence: to find out if something is working, you must isolate its effect. Controlled experimentation is inherently "marginal" in character.

Brailsford puts it this way: "If you break a performance into its component parts, you can build back up with confidence. Clear feedback is the cornerstone of improvement. Marginal gains, as an approach, is about having the intellectual honesty to see where you are going wrong, and delivering improvements as a result."

The marginal gains mentality has pervaded the entire Team Sky mindset. They make sure that the cyclists sleep on the same mattress each night to deliver a marginal gain in sleep quality; that the rooms are vacuumed before they arrive at each new hotel, to deliver a marginal gain in reduced infection; that the clothes are washed with skin-friendly detergent, a marginal gain in comfort.

"People think it is exhausting to think about success at such a high level of detail," Brailsford says. "But it would be far more exhausting, for me anyway, to neglect doing the analysis. I would much rather have clear answers than to delude myself that I have the 'right' answers."

• • •

Perhaps the most astonishing application of marginal gains is to be found not in cycling but in Formula One. In the closing weeks of the 2014 season I visited the Mercedes headquarters in Brackley, a few miles north of Oxford. It is a series of gray buildings on an industrial estate, with a stream running through it. It is populated with bright people, passionate about their sport—and whose attention to detail is staggering.

"When I first started in F1, we recorded eight channels of data. Now we have 16,000 from every single parameter on the car. And we derive another 50,000 channels from that data," said Paddy Lowe, a Cambridge-educated engineer, who is currently the technical leader of Mercedes F1. "Each channel provides information on a small aspect of performance. It takes us into the detail, but it also enables us to isolate key metrics that help us to improve."

The most intuitive way to glimpse the relationship between marginal gains and big achievements is to examine the pit stop. This is one of thousands of different components that, collectively, determine whether an F1 team is successful or not. It is a marginal aspect of performance, but a crucial one. In order to gain a deeper insight I went out to the season-ending Grand Prix in Abu Dhabi and immersed myself within the Mercedes operation.

At the team's motor home, a small, three-story house within the Yas Marina Circuit, I talked to James Vowles, chief strategist for Mercedes F1. I asked him how the team went about developing the optimum pit-stop procedure. Vowles says:

We use the same method for everything, not just pit stops. First of all, you need a decent understanding of the engineering problem. So, with the pit stops we came up with a strategy based on our blue-sky ideas. But this strategy was always going to be less than optimal, because the problem is complex. So we created sensors so we could measure what was happening and test our assumptions.

But the crucial thing is what happened next. Once you have gone through a practice cycle with the initial strategy, you immediately realize that there are miscellaneous items that you are not measuring. Just doing a pit-stop practice-run opens your eyes to data points that are relevant to the task, but that were absent from the initial blueprint. So the second stage of the cycle is about improving your measurement statistics, even before you start to improve the pit-stop process.

Think about that for a moment. We have talked about the concept of an open loop. This is where a strategy is put in action, then tested to see if it is working. By seeing what is going wrong, you can then improve the strategy. Mercedes takes this one step further. They use the first test not to improve the strategy, but to create richer feedback. Only when they have a deeper understanding of all the relevant data do they start to iterate.

Vowles says:

> We have placed eight sensors on every single one of the wheel-nut guns in order to access the most systematic data. Just by looking at this data, without speaking to the human involved, I can ascertain exactly what has happened on each pit stop. When the gun operator initially connected to the wheel nut, I can tell that they, say, connected 20 degrees off the optimum angle. When they start rotating the gun, I can tell how long it has taken for the nut to physically loosen all its preloaded torque and for the wheel to start moving off the axle.
>
> I can tell how quickly the gun man has moved away; how quickly he has reconnected, how long it has taken for the tire to be removed, the second tire to be refitted to the axle, how clean the second connection was to it, and how long he was gunning on for. The precision of this information helps us to create an optimization loop. It shows us how to improve every time-sensitive aspect.

This is marginal gains on turbocharge. "You improve your data set before you begin to improve your final function; what you are doing is ensuring that you have understood what you didn't initially understand," Vowles says. "This is important because you must have the right information at the right time in order to deliver the right optimization, which can further improve and guide the cycle."

Later that evening I went to the pit-lane to watch the team practice. It was an astonishing feat of collective endeavor. The car of Lewis Hamilton, the top driver for Mercedes, was pushed into position by three runners, and then instantly pounced upon by a team of around sixteen people, all with clearly defined tasks and exquisitely coordinated procedures. Again and again they practiced, dealing with every contingency that might arise in the race the next day. Every practice run was measured with the eight sensors, and videotaped, so it could pass through another optimization loop. One of the pit stops I witnessed was completed in an astonishing 1.95 seconds.[*]

Vowles said:

> The secret to modern F1 is not really to do with big ticket items; it is

about hundreds of thousands of small items, optimized to the nth degree. People think that things like engines are based upon high-level strategic decisions, but they are not. What is an engine except many iterations of small components? You start with a sensible design, but it is the iterative process that guides you to the best solution. Success is about creating the most effective optimization loop.

I also spoke to Andy Cowell, the leader of the team that devised the engine. His attitude was a carbon copy of that of Vowles.

We got our development engine up and running in late December [2012]. We didn't design it to be car friendly. We didn't try and figure out the perfect weight and aerodynamic design. Rather, we got a working model out there early, so that we could test it, and improve. It was the process of learning in the test cell that enabled us to create the most thermally efficient engine in the world.

The marginal gains approach is not just about mechanistic iteration. You need judgment and creativity to determine how to find solutions to what the data is telling you, but those judgments, in turn, are tested as part of the next optimization loop. Creativity not guided by a feedback mechanism is little more than white noise. Success is a complex interplay between creativity and measurement, the two operating together, the two sides of the optimization loop.

We will examine the creative process in more detail in the next chapter, but Vowles and Cowell have described a compelling model. It is the model used by Brailsford and the latest generation of development economists. Mercedes clocks up literally thousands of tiny failures. As Toto Wolff, the charismatic executive director of the team, put it: "We make sure we know where we are going wrong, so we can get things right."

The basic proposition of this book is that we have an allergic attitude to failure. We try to avoid it, cover it up, and airbrush it from our lives. We have looked at cognitive dissonance, the careful use of euphemisms, anything to divorce us from the pain we feel when we are confronted with the realization that we have underperformed.

Brailsford, Duflo and Vowles see weaknesses with a different set of eyes. Every error, every flaw, every failure, however small, is a marginal gain in disguise. This information is regarded not as a threat but as an opportunity. They are, in a sense, like aviation safety experts, who regard every near-miss event as a precious chance to avert an accident before it happens.*

On the eve of the Grand Prix at the Yas Marina Circuit, qualifying took place. This is where the drivers compete to see who can post the fastest lap, with the winner taking pole position (the most advantageous place on the starting grid) for the Grand Prix. Nico Rosberg, a German driver for Mercedes, took first place on the grid and Lewis Hamilton, his British teammate, took second place.

Afterward, I was given access to the highly secretive debriefing meeting. At a table in a room in the Mercedes garage, a few meters from the track, Hamilton and Rosberg sat facing each other. They were flanked by their respective race engineers. On the left was Paddy Lowe, the technical boss, and on other tables were experts in different aspects of performance.

Everybody wore headsets with microphones and scrutinized data on computer screens. On a big screen in the corner of the room was the team back in the UK, all hooked into the conversation. Much of the meeting was confidential. But the process was fascinating. Hamilton and Rosberg were taken through each dimension of performance: tires, engine, the helmet, whether the drinks provided during qualifying were at the right temperature.

Each observation from the two drivers was then double-checked against the hard data, and possible improvements noted. After the meeting, the next stage of the optimization loop was already underway, with analysts creating new marginal gains. I couldn't help contemplating the contrast between the spirit of this approach and that of other areas of our world.

The following day I observed the race from the Mercedes garage. Hamilton made a blistering start from second position on the grid and went on to win the race. The points from his victory propelled him to the overall driver's championship. Rosberg came in second in the overall classification. Mercedes won the constructors championship: the most successful team in F1.

Afterward, champagne bottles were uncorked in the garage as mechanics, engineers, pit-stop operators, and the two drivers finally let their hair down. "I drive the car, but I have an incredible operation behind me," Hamilton said. Vowles added: "We will enjoy tonight, but tomorrow we will feed what we learned today into the next stage of the optimization loop."

Paddy Lowe, the man responsible for the technical operation, looked on from the back of the garage. "F1 is an unusual environment because you have incredibly intelligent people driven by the desire to win," he said. "The ambition spurs rapid innovation. Things from just two years ago seem antique. Standing still is tantamount to extinction."

IV

Google had a decision to make. Jamie Divine, then one of the company's top designers, had come up with a new shade of blue to use on the Google toolbar. He reckoned it would boost the number of click-throughs.

The narrative surrounding the new shade sounded very good. The color was enticing; it meshed with what was known about consumer psychology. Divine, after all, was one of the top designers at the company. But how could Google be sure that he was right?

The conventional way would have been to change the color on the Google toolbar and see what happened. The obvious problem with this approach should, by now, be obvious. Even if clicks increased, Google could not be certain if the increase was caused by the color change or by something else. Perhaps the number of clicks would have gone up *even more* if the color had stayed the same.

And this is why, even as executives were debating Divine's shade, a product manager decided to conduct a test. He picked a slightly different shade of blue (one with a hint of green) and put it into a contest with the shade selected by Divine. In effect, users clicking on the Google website were randomly assigned to one of the two shades and their behavior monitored. It was an RCT. The result of the experiment was clear: more people clicked through on the blue with a hint of green.

There was no room for spin or bluster of the kind that often accompanies business decisions. There was just a flip of a coin, a random assignment, and a precise measurement.* The fact that Divine's shade lost out in this trial didn't mean he was a poor designer. Rather, it showed that his considerable knowledge was insufficient to predict how a tiny alteration in shade would impact consumer behavior. But then nobody could have known that for sure. The world is too complex.

But this was just the start. Google executives realized that the success of the greeny-blue shade was not conclusive. After all, who's to say that this particular shade is better than all other possible shades? Marissa Mayer, of Yahoo!, then a vice president at Google, came up with a more systematic trial. She divided the relevant part of the color spectrum into forty constituent shades and then ran another test.

Users of Google Mail were randomly grouped into forty populations of 2.5 percent and, as they visited the site at different times, were confronted with different shades, and tracked. Google was thus able to determine the optimal shade, not through blue-sky thinking or slick narratives, but through testing. They determined the optimum shade through trial and error.

This approach is now a key part of Google's operation. As of 2010, the company was carrying out 12,000 RCTs every year. This is an astonishing amount of experimentation and it means that Google clocks up thousands of little failures. Each RCT may seem like nitpicking, but the cumulative effect starts to look very different. According to Google UK's managing director, Dan Cobley, the color-switch generated $200 million in additional annual revenue.[*]

Perhaps the company most associated with randomized trials, however, is Capital One, the credit card provider. The business was created by Richard Fairbank and Nigel Morris, two consultants with backgrounds in evidence-based research. They created the company with one objective in mind: to test as widely and as intelligently as possible.

When sending out letters to solicit new clients, for example, they could have gone to a number of different experts who would doubtless have come up with different templates and colors. Should the color be red or blue? Should the font be Times New Roman or Calibri?

Instead of debating the questions, however, Fairbank and Morris tested them. They sent out 50,000 letters to randomly selected households with one color and 50,000 with another color, and then measured the relative profitability from the resulting groups. Then they tested different fonts, and different wording, and different scripts at their call centers.[9]

Every year since it was founded Capital One has run thousands of similar tests. They have turned the company into a "scientific laboratory where every decision about product design, marketing, channels of communication, credit lines, customer selection, collection policies, and cross-selling decisions could be subjected to systematic testing and using thousands of experiments."[10]

As of 2015, Capital One was valued at around £45 billion.

Jim Manzi, an American entrepreneur and author who helps companies to run randomized trials, estimates that 20 percent of all retail data is now put through his software platform. This hints, more than anything else, at how far the marginal gains approach has traveled in the corporate world. "Businesses now execute more RCTs than all other kinds of institutions combined," he told me. "It is one of the biggest changes in corporate practice for a generation."[11]

Harrah's Casino Group is symbolic of the quiet revolution that has been taking place. The brand, which operates casinos and resorts across America, reportedly has three golden rules for staff: "Don't harass women, don't steal, and you've got to have a control group."

· · ·

RCTs, whether in business or beyond, are often very dependent on context. A trial that improves, say, educational outcomes in Kenya has no claim to improve outcomes in London.[*] This is both the beauty of the social world, and its challenge. We need to run lots of trials, lots of replications, to tease out how far conclusions can be extended from one trial to other contexts. To do this we need to create the capacity for running experiments at scale and at a lower unit cost.

But this doesn't mean that we cannot draw big conclusions from RCTs. Perhaps the most ambitious use of randomized trials in public policy took place in regard to employment policy. In America in the 1980s, how to get people off welfare and into work was one of the most pressing issues of the day. Policy would conventionally have been decided by the top-down deliberations of presidents and congressmen in collaboration with advisers and pressure groups.

Instead, it was determined by experimentation. As Jim Manzi details in his excellent book *Uncontrolled*, states were given waivers to depart from federal policy on the proviso they used randomized trials to evaluate the changes. The results were dramatic. The trials revealed that financial incentives don't work. Time limits don't work.

The only thing that worked? Mandatory work requirements. This paved the way for Bill Clinton's highly successful workfare program, secured with the backing of a Republican Congress.

V

Marginal gains may seem like an approach that only big corporations, governments, and sports franchises can hope to adopt. After all, running controlled experiments requires expertise and, often, sizable budgets. But a willingness to test assumptions is ultimately about a mindset. It is about intellectual honesty and a readiness to learn when one fails. Seen in this way, it is relevant to any business; in fact to almost any problem.

Take Takeru Kobayashi. At one time, he was an impoverished economics student, struggling to pay the electric bill of the apartment he shared with his girlfriend in Yokkaichi, on the eastern coast of Japan. Then he heard about a televised speed-eating contest in the area that had a first prize of $5,000. He entered the competition, did a bit of serious practice, and won.[12]

Intrigued, he discovered that speed-eating is a globally competitive sport, with serious rewards. This was a possible route out of poverty. So, as documented in the excellent book *Think Like a Freak*, Kobayashi targeted the world's biggest competition—Nathan's Hot Dog Eating Contest, which takes place every July Fourth in Coney Island, New York.

The rules are straightforward: eat as many hot dogs and buns as you can in twelve minutes. You are allowed to drink anything you like, but you are not allowed to vomit significantly (a problem known in the sport as a "reversal of fortune").

Kobayashi approached the contest with a marginal gains mindset. First, instead of eating the hot dog as a whole (as all speed-eating champions had done until that point), he tried breaking it in half. He found that it gave him more options for chewing, and freed his hands to improve loading. It was a marginal gain. Then he experimented with eating the dog and the bread separately rather than at once. He found that the dogs went down super fast, but he still struggled with the chewy, doughy buns.

So he experimented by dipping the buns in water, then in water at different temperatures, then with water sprinkled with vegetable oil, then he videotaped his training sessions, recorded the data on spreadsheets, tracked slightly different strategies (flat out, pacing himself, sprint finishing), tested different ways of chewing, swallowing, and various "wriggles" that manipulated the space in his stomach in order to avoid vomiting. He tested each small assumption.

When he arrived at Coney Island he was a rank outsider. Nobody gave him a chance. He was slight and short, unlike many of his super-sized competitors. The world record was 25.125 hot dogs in twelve minutes, an astonishing total. Most observers thought this was close to the upper limit for humans. Kobayashi had other ideas. The student smashed the competition to pieces. He ate an eye-watering 50 hot dogs, almost doubling the record. "People think that if you have a huge appetite, then you'll be better at it," he said. "But, actually, it's how you confront the food that is brought to you."

Kobayashi had eaten more than any competitor in history not because he had a surgically enlarged stomach or an extra esophagus (as some competitors alleged); rather, he triumphed via the aggregation of marginal gains. By failing in all sorts of small, well-measured, rigorously tested ways, he iterated his way to success. It was bottom-up rather than top-down, if you'll forgive the expression.

And if this approach can be applied to eating salty tubes of sandwich meat, it can be applied to almost anything.

VI

To conclude this chapter, let's examine the concept of marginal gains in visual form. The process of optimization can be compared to trying to get to the top of a summit. Suppose you start from a position below the summit of the smaller of two hills, Point A, and take a tiny step in a particular direction. You then test to see if you have gone up and, if you have, you take another small step, and test again.

In this way, by taking lots of small steps, each rigorously examined to see if it is taking you in the right direction, you will eventually end up at the smaller summit. Indeed, this method is so powerful that it will work even if you are wearing a blindfold, as the business expert Eric Ries has written in an excellent essay on the art of optimization.[13]

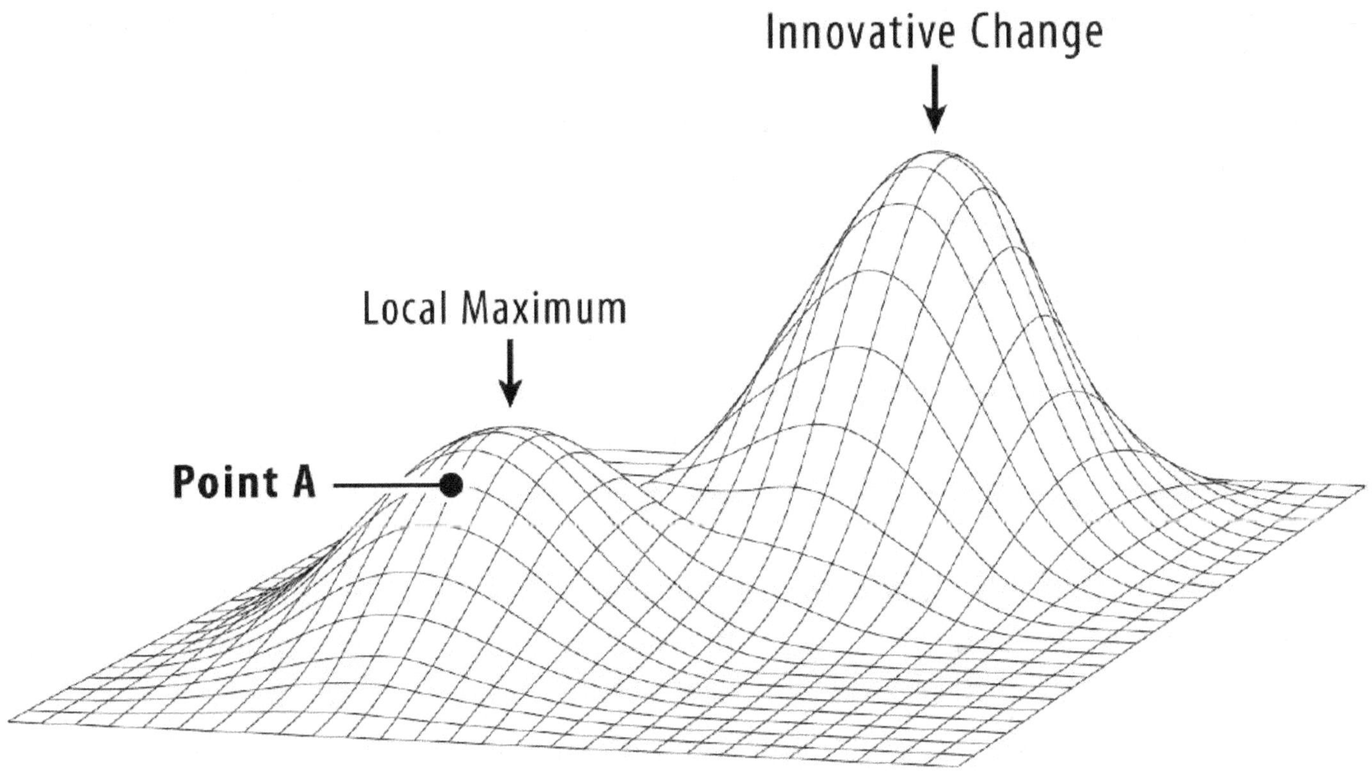

This is the potency of marginal gains. By dividing a big challenge into small parts, you are able to create rigorous tests, and thus deliver incremental improvements. Each may seem small or, as Brailsford often says, "virtually negligible," but over time, and with discipline, they accumulate. You eventually reach the optimum point, the summit of the smaller hill. This is the Local Maximum.[14] It is often the difference between winning and losing, whether in sports, business, or speed-eating hot dogs.

But this visualization also reveals the inherent limitations of marginal gains. Often in business, technology, and life, progress is not about small, well-delivered steps, but creative leaps. It is about acts of imagination that can transform the entire landscape of a problem. Indeed, these are sometimes the most important drivers of change in the modern world.

To see this difference, take Blockbuster. This was a business based around the renting of videos and later DVDs. As a concept it fared well for more than two decades, delivering an impressive rate of return. You can imagine a manager at the company using a marginal gains approach: altering the company's logo, tweaking the design of the shelving at the stores, trialing different discount approaches like two-for-one, and so on.

Each of these tests would have been useful. Over time they would have accumulated, taking the company toward the top of the local optimization summit. But the problem is also obvious: the business model was eventually superseded by Netflix and the like, rendering videos and DVDs, to a large extent, obsolete.* The entire landscape fundamentally changed. And no amount of marginal gains (at least within a realistic time frame) would have helped Blockbuster to survive. The company was liquidated in 2013.*

In the diagram, the new landscape is represented by the taller hill. Marginal gains is a strategy of local optimization: it takes you to the summit of the first hill. But once you are there, taking little steps, however well tested, runs out of traction. To have stayed ahead of the competition, Blockbuster would have needed to move into an entirely new space, leveraging new technology and fresh insights.

There is an ongoing debate in the political, scientific, and business worlds about whether to focus on the bold leaps that lead to new conceptual terrain, or on the marginal gains that help to optimize one's existing fundamental assumptions. Is it about testing small assumptions or big ones; is it about transforming the world or tweaking it; is it about considering the big picture (the so-called gestalt) or the fine detail (the margins)?

The simple answer, however, is that it has to be both. At the level of the system and, increasingly, at the level of the organization, success is about developing the capacity to think big and small, to be both imaginative and disciplined, to immerse oneself in the minutiae of a problem and to stand beyond it in order to glimpse the wider vista.

In this chapter we have looked at small steps and found that they are driven by discovering little failures. Marginal gains, as a philosophy, absolutely depends on the ability to detect and learn from small, often latent weaknesses. Now we are going to look at giant leaps, the audacious changes in technology, design, and science that transform our world.

And we will see that beneath the inspirational stories told about these shifts, the deepest and most overlooked truth is that innovation cannot happen without failure. Indeed, the aversion to failure is the single largest obstacle to creative change, not just in business but beyond.

Chapter 10

How Failure Drives Innovation

I

The headquarters of Dyson are in a futuristic building about forty miles west of Oxford. Outside the front entrance is a Harrier jump jet—not a replica, a real one—and a high-speed landing craft. They both hint at the unconventionality of what goes on inside.

James Dyson, the chairman and chief engineer of the company, works in a glass-fronted office just above the entrance. Along the back wall are the beautifully conceived products that have turned him into an icon of British innovation: super-efficient vacuum cleaners, futuristic hand dryers, and other devices yet to roll off the production line. In all, he has applied for more than four thousand patents.[1]

Progress is often driven not by the accumulation of small steps, but by dramatic leaps. The television wasn't an iteration of a previous device, it was a new technology altogether. Einstein's general theory of relativity didn't tinker with Newton's law of universal gravitation, it replaced it in almost every detail. Likewise Dyson's dual-cyclone vacuum cleaner was not a marginal improvement on the conventional Hoover that existed at the time, it represented a shift that altered the way insiders think about the very problem of removing dust and hair from household floors.

Dyson is an evangelist for the creative process of change, not least because he believes it is fundamentally misconceived in the world today. As we talk in his office, he darts around picking up papers, patents, textbooks, and his own designs to illustrate his argument. He is tall, bright-eyed, and restless. A conversation scheduled for half an hour continues late into the evening, so that by the end the sun has gone down, and his expressive face is lit only by a table lamp (designed, incidentally, by his son: it contains an LED light that lasts for 160,000 hours rather than the usual 2,000).

He says:

People think of creativity as a mystical process. The idea is that creative insights emerge from the ether, through pure contemplation. This model conceives of innovation as something that happens to people, normally geniuses. But this could not be more wrong. Creativity is something that has to be worked at, and it has specific characteristics. Unless we understand how it happens, we will not improve our creativity, as a society or as a world.

Dyson's journey into the nature of creativity started while vacuuming his own home, a small farmhouse in the west of England, on a Saturday morning in his mid-twenties. Like everyone else he was struck by just how quickly his cleaner lost suction. "It was a top-of-the-range Hoover," he says. "It had one of the most powerful vacuum motors in the world. But it lost its suction within minutes. It started to let out this high-pitched scream. I had faced the problem before. Growing up, it had been my chore to vacuum the family home and the suction was a constant bugbear. But this time I just snapped."

Dyson strode into his garden and opened up the device. Inside he could see the basic engineering proposition of the conventional vacuum cleaner: a motor, a bag (which also doubled as a filter), and a tube. The logic was simple: dust and air is sucked into the bag, the air escapes through the small holes in the lining of the bag and into the motor, and the dust (thicker than the air) stays in the bag. He says:

The bag was full of dust and so I assumed this was the reason that it had lost suction. So I ripped open the bag, emptied out the dust and Sellotaped it back up again. But when I went back to vacuum in the house, the efficiency was no better. The screaming started straight away. There was no suction.

I suddenly realized that the real problem was not that the bag was full; it was the thin lining of dust on the inside of the bag. The walls of the bag were clogged. The fine dust was blocking the filter. And that is why performance in conventional vacuum cleaners dips so rapidly; it is the very first dust that blocks them up.

This realization triggered a new thought: What if there were no bag? What if you could make an entirely bagless vacuum cleaner? "If you could find a way of removing the dust from the air another way, without using a conventional bag, you would no longer lose suction because of a blocked filter," he says. "It would revolutionize vacuum cleaning."

This idea percolated in Dyson's mind for the next three years. A graduate of the Royal College of Art, he was already a qualified engineer and was helping to run a local company in Bath. He enjoyed pulling things apart and seeing how they worked. He was curious, inquisitive, and willing to engage with a difficulty rather than just accepting it. But now he had a live problem, one that intrigued him.

It wasn't until he went to a lumberyard that the solution powered into his mind like a thunderbolt.

Nowadays you pick up wood from a merchant and just walk out. In the old days, they virtually had to cut and plane it for you. There was a lot of hanging about. As I stood there waiting I noticed this ducting going off the machines. It traveled along to this thing on the roof, thirty or forty foot tall.

It was a cyclone [a cone-shaped device that changes the dynamics of the airflow, separating the dust from the air via centrifugal force]. It was made of galvanized steel. And although a ton of dust was coming off the machines as they cut the wood, there was no dust coming out of the chimney at the top. I was intrigued. This thing was collecting fine dust all day long and it didn't look as though it was blocking at all.

Dyson rushed home. This was his moment of insight. "I vaguely knew about cyclones, but not really the detail. But I was fascinated to see if it would work in miniature form. I got an old cardboard box and made a replica of what I had seen with gaffer tape and cardboard. I then connected it via a bit of hose to an upright vacuum cleaner. And I had my cardboard cyclone."

His heart was beating fast as he pushed it around the house. Would it work? "It seemed absolutely fine," he says. "It seemed to be picking up dust, but the dust didn't seem to be coming out of the chimney. I went to my boss and said: 'I think I have an interesting idea.'"

This simple idea, this moment of insight, would ultimately make Dyson a personal fortune in excess of £3 billion.

II

A number of things jump out about the Dyson story. The first is that the solution seems rather obvious in hindsight. This is often the case with innovation, and it's something we will come back to.

But now consider a couple of other aspects of the story. The first is that the creative process started with a *problem,* what you might even call a failure, in the existing technology. The vacuum cleaner kept blocking. It let out a screaming noise. Dyson had to keep bending down to pick up bits of trash by hand.

Had everything been going smoothly Dyson would have had no motivation to change things. Moreover, he would have had no intellectual challenge to sink his teeth into. It was the very nature of the engineering problem that sparked a possible solution (a bagless vacuum cleaner).

And this turns out to be an almost perfect metaphor for the creative process, whether it involves vacuum cleaners, a quest for a new brand name, or a new scientific theory. Creativity is, in many respects, a *response.*

Relativity was a response to the failure of Newtonian mechanics to make accurate predictions when objects were moving at fast speeds.

Masking tape was a response to the failure of existing adhesive tape, which would rip the paint off when it was removed from cars and walls.

The collapsible stroller was a response to the impracticality of unwieldy baby carriages (Owen Maclaren, the designer, came up with the idea after watching his daughter struggling with a baby carriage while out with his granddaughter).

The wind-up radio was a response to the lack of batteries in Africa, something that was hampering the spread of educational information (Trevor Baylis came up with the idea after watching a television program on AIDS).

The ATM was a response to the problem of getting hold of cash outside of business hours. It was invented by John Shepherd-Barron while lying in the bath one night, worrying because he had forgotten to go to the bank.

Dropbox, as we have seen, was a response to the problem of forgetting your flash drive and thus not having access to important files.

This aspect of the creative process, the fact that it emerges in response to a particular difficulty, has spawned its own terminology. It is called the "problem phase" of innovation. "The damn thing had been bugging me for years," Dyson says of the conventional vacuum cleaner. "I couldn't bear the inefficiency of the technology. It wasn't so much a 'problem phase' as a 'hatred phase.'"

We often leave this aspect of the creative process out of the picture. We focus on the moment of epiphany, the detonation of insight that happened when Newton was hit by the apple or Archimedes was taking a bath. That is perhaps why creativity seems so ethereal. The idea is that such insights could happen anytime, anywhere. It is just a matter of sitting back and letting them flow.

But this leaves out an indispensable feature of creativity. Without a problem, without a failure, without a flaw, without a frustration, innovation has nothing to latch on to. It loses its pivot. As Dyson puts it: "Creativity should be thought of as a dialogue. You have to have a problem before you can have the game-changing riposte."

Perhaps the most graphic way to glimpse the responsive nature of creativity is to consider an experiment by Charlan Nemeth, a psychologist at the University of California, Berkeley, and her colleagues.[2] She took 265 female undergraduates and randomly divided them into five-person teams. Each team was given the same task: to come up with ideas about how to reduce traffic congestion in the San Francisco Bay Area. These five-person teams were then assigned to one of three ways of working.

The first group were given the instruction to brainstorm. This is one of the most influential creativity techniques in history, and it is based on the mystical conception of how creativity happens: through contemplation and the free flow of ideas. In brainstorming the entire approach is to *remove* obstacles. It is to minimize challenges. People are warned not to criticize each other, or point out the difficulties in each other's suggestions. Blockages are bad. Negative feedback is a sin.

As Alex Faickney Osborn, an advertising executive who wrote a series of best-selling books on brainstorming in the 1940s and 1950s, put it: "Creativity is so delicate a flower that praise tends to make it bloom, while discouragement often nips it in the bud."[3]

The second group were given no guidelines at all: they were allowed to come up with ideas in any way they thought best.

But the third group were actively encouraged to point out the flaws in each other's ideas. Their instructions read: "Most research and advice suggests that the best way to come up with good solutions is to come up with many solutions. Free-wheeling is welcome; don't be afraid to say anything that comes to mind. However, in addition, most studies suggest that *you should debate and even criticize each other's ideas* [my italics]."

The results were remarkable. The groups with the dissent and criticize guidelines generated 25 percent more ideas than those who were brainstorming (or who had no instructions). Just as striking, when individuals were later asked to come up with more solutions for the traffic problem, those with the dissent guidelines generated twice as many new ideas as the brainstormers.

Further studies have shown that those who dissent rather than brainstorm produce not just more ideas, but more productive and imaginative ideas. As Nemeth put it: "The basic finding is that the encouragement of debate—and even criticism if warranted—appears to stimulate more creative ideas. And cultures that permit and even encourage such expression of differing viewpoints may stimulate the most innovation."

The reason is not difficult to identify. The problem with brainstorming is not its insistence on free-wheeling or quick association. Rather, it is that when these ideas are not checked by the feedback of criticism, they have nothing to respond to. Criticism surfaces problems. It brings difficulties to light. This forces us to think afresh. When our assumptions are violated we are nudged into a new relationship with reality. Removing failure from innovation is like removing oxygen from a fire.

Think back to Dyson and his Hoover. It was the flaw in the existing technology that forced Dyson to think about cleaning in a new way. The blockage in the filter wasn't something to hide away from or pretend wasn't there. Rather, the blockage, the failure, was a gilt-edged invitation to reimagine vacuum-cleaning.

Imagination is not fragile. It feeds off flaws, difficulties, and problems. Insulating ourselves from failures—whether via brainstorming guidelines, the familiar cultural taboo on criticism, or the influence of cognitive dissonance*— is to rob one of our most valuable mental faculties of fuel.

"It always starts with a problem," Dyson says. "I hated vacuum cleaners for twenty years, but I hated hand dryers for even longer. If they had worked perfectly, I would have had no motivation to come up with a new solution. But more important, I would not have had the context to offer a creative solution. Failures feed the imagination. You cannot have the one without the other."

Perhaps the most eloquent testimony to the creative power of error comes from a different experiment by Nemeth and a colleague.[4] In a typical free association study, we are given a word and have to respond with the first word that pops into our heads.

The problem is that when many of us free-associate, we come up with rather boring associations. If someone says "blue," most people reply "sky." If someone says "green," we say "grass." This is hardly the stuff of inspiration. In her free-association experiment, Nemeth showed slides to volunteers. As expected, they came up with conventional, banal associations.

But then she had a lab assistant call out the wrong color as part of the experiment. When a blue slide was shown, the assistant called out "green." And this is when something odd happened. When Nemeth then asked these volunteers to free-associate on the colors that had been wrongly identified, they suddenly became far more creative. They came up with associations that reached way beyond tired convention. Blue became "jeans" or "lonely" or "Miles Davis."[5]

What was going on? We should now be able to glimpse an answer. Contradictory information *jars,* in much the same way that error jars. It encourages us to engage in a new way. We start to reach beyond our usual thought processes (why would you think differently when things are going just as expected?). When someone shouts out the wrong color, our conventional mental operations are disrupted. That is when we find associations, connections, that might never have occurred to us.

And this takes us to the second crucial aspect of the Dyson story. You'll remember that in his moment of insight he essentially brought two disparate ideas together: a vacuum cleaner and a sawmill. These were two different things. They existed in two different places of vastly different scale: in the home and in the sawmill. You could almost say that they inhabited separate conceptual categories.

Dyson's innovation, stripped down to its essentials, was to merge them. He was a *connecting agent.* The act of creativity was an act, above all, of synthesis. "I think the fact that I had so many years of frustration probably made me the perfect person to glimpse a possible solution," he says. "But the solution was really about combining two existing technologies."

And it turns out that this act of connectivity is another central feature of innovation. Johannes Gutenberg invented mass printing by applying the pressing of wine (the technology of which had existed for many centuries) to the pressing of pages.[6]

The Wright brothers applied their understanding of manufacturing bicycles to the problem of powered flight.

The rank algorithm behind the success of Google was developed by Sergey Brin and Larry Page from an existing method of ranking academic articles.

Sellotape, a staggeringly successful commercial innovation, was developed by merging glue and cellophane.

The collapsible stroller was created by fusing the folding undercarriages for Spitfires in the Second World War with an existing technology for transporting children.

Little wonder that Steve Jobs, a master in the art of merging concepts, once said: "Creativity is just connecting things."

If failure sparks creativity into life, the moment of insight invariably emerges from the attempt to bridge the problem with previously unconnected ideas or technologies. It is about finding a hidden connection in order to solve a problem with meaning. But the crucial point to realize is that these processes are intimately intertwined. It is precisely because we have been hit by jarring information that we are nudged into looking for unusual connections, as we saw in the free association experiment.

To put it simply, failure and epiphany are inextricably linked. When we come up with a brilliant idea, when it pops into our mind, it has often emerged from a period of gestation. It is a consequence of engaging with a problem, sometimes, as in the case of Dyson, for many years.

As the neuroscientist David Eagleman says in his book *Incognito: The Secret Lives of the Brain*: "When an idea is served up from behind the scenes, the neural circuitry has been working on the problems for hours or days or years, consolidating information and trying out new combinations. But you merely take credit without further wonderment at the vast, hidden political machinery behind the scenes."[7]

Much of the literature on creativity focuses on how to trigger these moments of innovative synthesis; how to drive the problem phase toward its resolution. And it turns out that epiphanies often happen when we are in one of two types of environment.

The first is when we are switching off: having a shower, going for a walk, sipping a cold beer, daydreaming. When we are too focused, when we are thinking too literally, we can't spot the obscure associations that are so important to creativity. We have to take a step back for the "associative state" to emerge. As the poet Julia Cameron put it: "I learned to get out of the way and let that creative force work through me."[8]

The other type of environment where creative moments often happen, as we have seen, is when we are being sparked by the dissent of others. When Kevin Dunbar, a psychologist at McGill University, went to look at how scientific breakthroughs actually happen, for example (he took cameras into four molecular biology labs and recorded pretty much everything that took place), he assumed that it would involve scientists beavering away in isolated contemplation.

In fact, the breakthroughs happened at lab meetings, where groups of researchers would gather around a desk to talk through their work. Why here? Because they were forced to respond to challenges and critiques from their fellow researchers. They were jarred into seeing new associations.

As the author Steven Johnson puts it: "Questions from colleagues forced researchers to think about their experiments on a different scale or level. Group interactions challenged researchers" assumptions about their more surprising findings . . . The ground zero of innovation was not the microscope. It was the conference table."[9]

And this helps to explain why cities are so creative, why atriums are important; in fact why any environment that allows disparate people, and therefore ideas, to bump into each other, is so conducive. They facilitate the association of diverse ideas, and bring people face-to-face with dissent and criticism. All help to ignite creativity.

● ● ●

This brief jaunt through the literature on creativity reveals one thing above all else: innovation is highly *context-dependent*. It is a response to a particular problem at a particular time and place. Take away the context, and you remove both the spur to innovation, and its raw material.

The best way to see this truth is through the phenomenon of *the multiple.* Steven Johnson runs through an entire list of breakthroughs that were conceived by different people, working independently, at almost precisely the same time.[10]

Sunspots, for example, were discovered by four scientists in four different countries in 1611. The mathematical calculus was developed by both Sir Isaac Newton and Gottfried Leibniz in the 1670s. The forerunner to the first electric battery was invented by Ewald Georg von Kleist in 1745 and Andreas Cuneus of Leyden in 1746.

Four people independently proposed the law of the conservation of energy in the 1840s. The theory of evolution through natural selection was proposed independently by Charles Darwin and Alfred Russel Wallace (an extraordinary, unsung polymath) in the mid-nineteenth century.[11] S. Korschinsky in 1889 and Hugo de Vries in 1901 independently established the significance of genetic mutation.

Even Einstein's pioneering work has echoes in the work of his contemporaries. The French mathematician Henri Poincaré wrote about the "Principle of Relativity" in 1904, a year before Einstein published his landmark paper on the Special Theory.

In the 1920s William Ogburn and Dorothy Thomas, two academics from Columbia University, found as many as 148 examples of independent innovation. Multiples are the norm; not the exception. They entitled their paper "Are Inventions Inevitable?"[*]

The reason harks back to the "responsive" nature of creativity. The failures of Newton's Laws created a specific problem. It invited particular solutions. It wasn't just Einstein and Poincaré, but also Hendrik Lorentz and David Hilbert who were working on a possible remedy.[12] Indeed, the so-called relativity priority dispute is about who invented what, when.[13]

And that is why the seductive idea that if Einstein had been born three hundred years earlier, we could have had the benefit of the theory of relativity in the seventeenth century is so flawed. Relativity *couldn't* have happened back then, largely because the problems that it responded to were not yet visible.

Einstein may have seen further and deeper than his contemporaries (there is still a large role for individualism: Einstein really was a creative genius), but he wasn't pulling insights out of the ether. As Johnson writes: "Good ideas are not conjured out of thin air."

Dyson is well aware of this aspect of creativity. "Every time I have gone for a patent in a particular field, someone else has got there first," he says. "I don't think there has been a single time in all the thousands of patents we have applied for where we were the first. With the vacuum cyclone, there were already a number of patents lodged."

But this raises a rather obvious question. Why didn't the person who came up with the original idea for a vacuum cyclone go on to make a fortune (the first cyclone vacuum-cleaner patent was lodged as early as 1928[14])? Why did Dyson, rather than his predecessors, change the world of domestic cleaning?

We noted earlier that we tend to overlook what happens *before* the moment of epiphany. But, if anything, we are even more neglectful of what happens afterward. This is a serious oversight because it obscures the reason why some people change the world while others are footnotes in the patent catalog.

The eureka moment is not the endpoint of innovation, it is the start of perhaps the most fascinating stage of all.

III

Dyson strode into his workshop. He had come up with his big idea: a bagless vacuum cleaner where dust is removed from the air by the geometry of the airflow rather than a filter. But he was pretty much alone. The directors at his company didn't back his idea (the response he received was: "If that is such a good concept, how come Hoover and Electrolux aren't doing it already?"), so he started his own business along with a silent partner, who had provided half the capital.

Dyson's workshop was a tiny former coach house. It had no windows and no heating. At the beginning he had no tools and precious little money. He also had huge debts, having remortgaged his house in order to start the business. But the then thirty-three-year-old (who also had three young children—and a very understanding wife) was nothing if not determined.

His first prototype, as we have seen, was the cardboard-and-gaffer-tape cyclone that he made after returning from the lumberyard. It seemed to work well. But although no dust was visible to the naked eye coming out of the top of the makeshift cyclone, he had to check whether he was getting rid of *all* the dust.

This was one of his first post-epiphany tasks. He bought some black cloth and obtained a quantity of fine white dust. Then he placed the cloth above his makeshift cyclone, vacuumed the dust, and noticed that some of it was, indeed, getting through. He could see white residue on the cloth.

So he altered the dimensions of the cyclone to see if it would improve the efficiency. He tried new sizes, new shapes. Each time he would note how a small change in one dimension would impact the overall engineering solution. The key challenge was to balance airflow with separation efficiency.

With each iteration he was learning new things. He was seeing what worked. Most of the time he was failing. "A cyclone has a number of variables: size of entry, exit, angle, diameter, length: and the trying thing is that if you change one dimension, it affects all the others."

His discipline was astonishing. "I couldn't afford a computer, so I would hand-write the results into a book," he recalls. "In the first year alone, I conducted literally hundreds of experiments. It was a very, very thick book."

But as the intensive, iterative process gradually solved the problem of separating ultra-fine dust, Dyson came up against another problem: long pieces of hair and fluff. These were not being separated from the airflow by the cyclone dynamics. "They were just coming out of the top along with the air," he says. "It was another huge problem and it didn't seem as if a conventional cyclone could solve it."

The sheer scale of the problem set the stage for a second eureka moment: the dual cyclone. "The first cyclone gets rid of the awkward strands of cotton or hair, before the air is pushed into the second cyclone, which gets rid of the finer dust," he went on. "You need both to make the device work properly."

In all, it took an astonishing 5,127 prototypes before Dyson believed the technology was ready to go in the vacuum cleaner. The creative leap may have been a crucial and precious thing, but it was only the start of the creative process. The real hard yards were done patiently evolving the design via bottom-up iteration. To put it another way, with the epiphany he had vaulted onto a taller mountain in a new landscape; now he was systematically working toward this new summit.

According to Dyson:

When you file a patent, somebody is almost always there before you. A lot of your argument with the patent examiner is to say: "Look, they may have had the eureka moment when they came back from the timber yard. They may even have created an early prototype." But none of my forebears had made their prototypes work. Mine is statistically different. That was my decisive advantage.

Creativity, then, has a dual aspect. Insight often requires taking a step back and seeing the big picture. It is about drawing together disparate ideas. It is the art of *connection*. But to make a creative insight work requires disciplined focus. As Dyson puts it: "If insight is about the big picture, development is about the small picture. The trick is to sustain both perspectives at the same time."

And this turns out to be the very cornerstone of understanding how creative success happens in the world today, as alluded to at the end of the last chapter. It is often said that in a rapidly changing world innovative companies will dominate. But this is, at best, only partly true. In their book *Great by Choice*, Jim Collins and Morten Hansen show that innovation may indeed be a *necessary* condition for success, but it is by no means sufficient.[15]

Genentech, the U.S.-based biotechnology corporation, for example, outpaced Amgen, a major competitor, by more than two times in patent productivity between 1983 and 2002 (they also outpaced Amgen in terms of the impact of their patents as measured by the number of citations) but Amgen's financial performance outperformed that of Genentech by more than thirty to one.

This finding is by no means unusual. In their book *Will and Vision*, Gerard J. Tellis and Peter N. Golder looked at the relationship between long-term market leadership and pioneering innovation in sixty-six different commercial sectors. They found that only 9 percent of the pioneers ended up as the final winners. They also found that 64 percent of pioneers failed outright.[16]

Jim Collins writes: "Gillette didn't pioneer the safety razor, Star did. Polaroid didn't pioneer the instant camera, Dubroni did. Microsoft didn't pioneer the personal computer spreadsheet, VisiCorp did. Amazon didn't pioneer online bookselling and AOL didn't pioneer online Internet service."[17]

What was the key ingredient that characterized the winners, the companies that may not have come up with an idea first, but who made it work? The answer can be conveyed in one word: *discipline*. This is not just the discipline to iterate a creative idea into a rigorous solution; it is also the discipline to get the manufacturing process perfect, the supply lines faultless, and delivery seamless.[*]

Dyson was not the first to come up with the idea of a cyclone vacuum cleaner. He was not even the second, or the third. But he was the only one with the stamina to "fail" his concept into a workable solution. And he had the rigor to create an efficient manufacturing process, so he could sell a consistent product.

His competitors confronted the same problem and had the same insight. But they didn't have the same resilience to make their idea work, let alone take it on to a working production line.

Collins takes the battle between Intel and Advanced Memory Systems as symbolic of this crucial distinction. Intel was months behind its fierce competitor in the race for the 1,000-bit memory chip. In the rush to introduce the 1103 chip, it hit major problems, including one that could actually erase data from the chip. It was so far behind the game that the outcome seemed like a foregone conclusion.

And yet Intel destroyed Advanced Memory Systems in the marketplace. They worked around the clock, creating new prototypes, iterating the chip into a workable solution. But they also insured that they nailed all the surrounding supply issues crucial for success. As Collins puts it: "Intel obsessed over manufacturing, delivery and scale."

By 1973, everyone was using Intel. Its slogan is not "Intel Creates," it is "Intel Delivers."

Dyson says:

It is no good creating the most beautiful products if you produce them shoddily. It is no good having the most innovative engineering solution if the consumers can't be certain it will be delivered on time. It is no good if inconsistent production means that a great idea is not translated into a polished product. The original idea is only 2 percent of the journey. You mustn't neglect the rest.

Collins writes:

We concluded that each environment has a level of "threshold innovation" that you need to meet to be a contender in the game . . . Companies that fail even to meet the innovation threshold cannot win. But—and this surprised us—once you're above the threshold, especially in a highly turbulent environment, being more innovative doesn't seem to matter very much.[18]

Winners require innovation *and* discipline, the imagination to see the big picture and the focus to perceive the very small. "The great task, rarely achieved, is to blend creative intensity with relentless discipline so as to amplify the creativity rather than destroy it," Collins writes. "When you marry operating excellence with innovation, you multiply the value of your creativity."[19]

IV

et us conclude our study of creativity by looking at Pixar, an animation company
that draws together many of these strands. As an institution it has almost no peers in its reputation for innovation. When Ed Catmull, the company's long-serving president, wrote his autobiography he entitled it *Creativity Inc*.

Pixar blockbusters include *Toy Story*, *Monsters, Inc.*, and *Finding Nemo*. The films have generated an average worldwide gross of over $600 million. They have been critical successes, too, winning Oscars in multiple categories. *Toy Story* and *Toy Story 2* both received 100 percent scores on Rotten Tomatoes.

Naturally Pixar has a lot of clever, creative people working in its offices. Lead authors come up with terrific story lines for the latest film. They are presented to the wider group at large meetings. They are often applauded afterward. A good storyline is an act of creative synthesis: bringing disparate narrative strands together in novel form. It is a crucial part of the Pixar process.

But now consider what happens next. The story line is pulled apart. As the animation gets into operation, each frame, each strand of the story, each scene is subject to debate, dissent, and testing. All told, it takes around twelve thousand storyboard drawings to make one ninety-minute feature, and because of the iterative process, story teams often create more than 125,000 storyboards by the time the film is actually delivered.

Monsters, Inc. is a perfect illustration of a creative idea adapted in the light of criticism. It started off with a plot centered on a middle-aged accountant who hates his job and who is given a sketchbook by his mother. As a child he had drawn some monsters in the sketchbook and that night they turn up in his bedroom, but only the accountant can see them. These monsters become the fears he had never confronted, and over time he learns to understand them, and thus overcome them.

The final version, which would wow the world (and take $560 million at the box office), is rather different. It tells the story of Sulley, a rather unkempt monster, and his unlikely friendship with a little girl nicknamed Boo. Over the period of the film's development it was altered in the light of criticism and the testing of ideas. Even after the main protagonist had changed to a little girl rather than a middle-aged accountant, the plot continued to evolve. Catmull has written:

> The human protagonist was a six-year-old named Mary. Then she was seven, named Boo, and bossy—even domineering. Finally Boo was turned into a fearless, preverbal toddler. The idea of Sulley's buddy

character—the round, one-eyed Mike, voiced by Billy Crystal—wasn't added until more than a year after the first treatment was written. The process of determining the rules of the incredibly intricate world Pete [the director of the film] created also took him down countless blind alleys—until eventually those blind alleys converged on a path that led the story where it needed to go.[20]

Toy Story 2 is another archetype of the Pixar creative process. Just a year out from its theatrical release, the narrative was not right. The story is about whether Woody, a toy cowboy, will leave the pampered life he enjoys on the shelf of a collector to go back to Andy, whom he loves. The problem is that this is a Disney movie, and so the audience knows at the outset that it will have a happy ending: Woody will reunite with Andy.

"What the film needed were reasons to believe that Woody was facing a real dilemma, and one that viewers could relate to. What it needed, in other words, was drama," Catmull writes in his memoir. With the clock ticking, the process of iteration took on an urgent feel. People were working overtime, late into the night, testing ideas.

One artist turned up at work with his small child, intending to take him to day care, but forgot. After he had been at work a couple of hours, his wife phoned to ask how the drop-off had gone. Suddenly he realized that he'd left the child in the boiling-hot parking lot. They rushed out and poured cold water on the unconscious child. Thankfully he was OK, but the episode revealed how stretched the staff had become.

Hundreds of small changes were made to the film. Dozens of larger changes were made too. There was also one major alteration to the plot: the story had always started with Woody suffering a rip in his arm that meant Andy left him behind when going to cowboy camp. At this point there was a decision to add a new character.

"[We] added a character named Wheezy the penguin, who tells Woody that he has been on that same shelf for months because of a broken squeaker," Catmull says. "Wheezy introduces the idea early on that no matter how cherished, when a toy gets damaged, it is likely to be shelved, tossed aside— maybe for good. Wheezy, then, establishes the emotional stakes of the story."

The plot now had real tension. Will Woody stay with someone he loves, knowing he will eventually be discarded, or choose a world where he can be pampered forever? It is a theme with high crossover and moral seriousness.

Ultimately, Woody chooses Andy but in the foreknowledge that the decision will lead to future unhappiness. "I can't stop Andy from growing up," he says to Stinky Pete. "But I wouldn't miss it for the world."

Catmull says:

> Early on, all of our movies suck. That's a blunt assessment, I know, but I . . . choose that phrasing because saying it in a softer way fails to convey how bad the first versions of our films really are. I'm not trying to be modest or self-effacing by saying this. Pixar films are not good at first, and our job is to make them go . . . from suck to non-suck . . .
>
> We are true believers in the power of bracing, candid feedback and the iterative process—reworking, reworking and reworking again, until a flawed story finds its throughline or a hollow character finds its soul.

Does this sound familiar? It is an almost perfect description of the dissent guidelines in the Nemeth experiment.

It is sometimes said that testing may be important for engineers and hard items like vacuum cleaners, nozzles, and curtain rods, but it doesn't apply to soft, intangible problems like writing novels or scripts for children's animations. In fact, iteration is vital for both. It is not an optional extra; it is an indispensable aspect of the creative process.

Consider what happened when Pixar considered abandoning its iron discipline; when they tried to go from epiphany to final product in one large, mystical leap. "This then became our goal—finalize the script *before* we start making the film," Catmull writes about *Finding Nemo*. "We were confident that locking in the story early would yield not just a phenomenal movie but a cost-efficient production."

It didn't work. The initial idea by Andrew Stanton, one of Pixar's most respected directors, was about an overprotective clownfish called Marlin, looking for his son. His pitch to the team was superb. "The narrative, as he described it, would be intercut with a series of flashbacks that explained what had happened to make Nemo's father such an overprotective worrywart when it came to his son," Catmull writes. "He seamlessly wove together two stories: what was happening in Marlin's world, during the epic search after Nemo is scooped up by a scuba diver, and what was happening in the aquarium in Sydney, where Nemo had ended up with a group of tropical fish called 'the Tank Gang.'"

The response in the room was one of stunned admiration. But once the creative blueprint was put into production, flaws began to emerge. The flashbacks proved confusing to test audiences. Marlin seemed unlikable because it took so long to see why he had been so overprotective. When Michael Eisner of Disney saw the rough cut he was not impressed. "Yesterday we saw for the second time the next Pixar movie *Finding Nemo*. It's OK, but nowhere near as good as their previous films."

At this point Pixar reverted to disciplined iteration. First they adapted the narrative to a more chronological approach—and it began to align. The tale of the Tank Gang became a subplot. Other changes, smaller, but cumulatively significant, began to emerge. By the end, the film had gone from suck to non-suck. Catmull writes:

> Despite our hopes that *Finding Nemo* would be the film that changed the way we did business, we ended up making as many adjustments during production as we had on any other film we had made. The result, of course, was a movie we're incredibly proud of, one that went on to become the highest grossing animated film ever.
>
> The only thing it didn't do was transform our production process.[21]

V

Dyson, Catmull, and the other innovators we have encountered offer a powerful rebuke to the way we conventionally think about creativity. To spark the imagination and take our insights to their fullest expression, we should not insulate ourselves from failure; rather, we should engage with it.

This perspective does not only have large implications for innovation, it also has direct implications for the way we teach. Today education is conceived as providing young people with a body of knowledge. Students are rewarded when they apply this knowledge correctly. Failures are punished.

But this is surely only one part of how we learn. We learn not just by being correct, but also by being wrong. It is when we fail that we learn new things, push the boundaries, and become more creative. Nobody had a new insight by regurgitating information, however sophisticated.

Dyson says:

We live in a world of experts. There is nothing particularly wrong with that. The expertise we have developed is crucial for all of us. But when we are trying to solve new problems, in business or technology, we need to reach beyond our current expertise. We do not want to know how to *apply* the rules; we want to *break* the rules. We do that by failing—and learning.

Dyson advocates that we provide children with the tools they need not just to answer questions, but to ask questions. "The problem with academia is that it is about being good at remembering things like chemical formulae and theories, because that is what you have to regurgitate. But children are not allowed to learn through experimenting and experience. This is a great pity. You need both."

One of the most powerful aspects of the Dyson story is that it evokes a point that was made in chapter 7; namely, that technological change is often driven by the synergy between practical and theoretical knowledge. One of the first things Dyson did when he had the insight for a cyclone cleaner was to buy two books on the mathematical theory of how cyclones work. He also went to visit the author of one of those books, an academic named R. G. Dorman.[22]

This was hugely helpful to Dyson. It allowed him to understand cyclone dynamics more fully. It played a role in directing his research and gave him a powerful background on the mathematics of separation efficiency. But it was by no means sufficient. The theory was too abstract to lead him directly to the precise dimensions that would deliver a functional vacuum cleaner.

Moreover, as Dyson iterated his device, he discovered that the theory had flaws. Dorman's equation predicted that cyclones would only be able to remove fine dust down to a lower limit of 20 microns. But Dyson quickly broke through this theoretical limit. By the end, his cyclone could separate dust smaller than 0.3 micron (this is approximately the size of the particles in cigarette smoke). Dyson's practical engagement with the problem had forced a change in the theory.

And this is invariably how progress happens. It is an interplay between the practical and the theoretical, between top-down and bottom-up, between creativity and discipline, between the small picture and the big picture. The crucial point—and the one that is most dramatically overlooked in our culture—is that in all these things, failure is a blessing, not a curse. It is the jolt that inspires creativity and the selection test that drives evolution.

Failure has many dimensions, many subtle meanings, but unless we see it in a new light, as a friend rather than a foe, it will remain woefully underexploited. Andrew Stanton, director of *Finding Nemo* and *WALL-E*, has said:

My strategy has always been: be wrong as fast as we can . . . which basically means, we're gonna screw up, let's just admit that. Let's not be afraid of that. But let's do it as fast as we can so we can get to the answer. You can't get to adulthood before you go through puberty. I won't get it right the first time, but I will get it wrong really soon, really quickly.

As our conversation draws to a close, I wonder why Dyson still comes into his office every day, rather than enjoying his wealth. "A lot of people ask me that. They seem to assume that I spend my life with my feet up," he says, smiling.

But the answer is simple: I love the creative process. I love coming in here every day and testing new ideas. We have plans for many new products in the coming years.

But we are also still developing the vacuum cleaner. We didn't stop at the 5,127th prototype, you know. Today, we have forty-eight cyclone technology, which spins the dust at 200,000 Gs. It exerts a huge centrifugal force, which is why it can separate the tiniest particles. But even this isn't the end. What excites me most is that we are still only at the beginning.